BRICKS & MORTAR OUGHTA

What **Real World** Businesses Can Learn from the **Internet**

JOHN W. HAYES

R & D Business Publishing
Unit 3, Cleethorpes Business Centre,
Jackson Place,
Grimsby,
North East Lincolnshire.
DN36 4AS.

First published in Great Britain in 2015

Copyright © John W. Hayes

The right of John W. Hayes to be identified as the Author has been asserted in accordance with the Copyright, Design and Patents Act 1988.

All rights reserved; no part of this publication may be reproduced, stored in a retrieval system or transmitted in any form or by any means, electronic, mechanical, photocopying, recording or otherwise without the prior written permission of the Publisher. This book may not be lent, resold, hired out or otherwise disposed of by way of trade in any form of binding or cover other than that in which it is published, without the prior written consent of the Publisher.

No responsibility for loss occasioned to any person or corporate body acting or refraining to act as a result of reading material in this book can be accepted by the Publisher, by the Author, or by the employer(s) of the Author.

ISBN-978-1505433142

CONTENTS

ABOUT THE AUTHOR   1

PREFACE   3

WHO IS THIS BOOK FOR?   7

CHAPTER 1 – FIRST IMPRESSIONS COUNT   9
- The Online Advantage   9
- 8 Lazy Retail Mistakes That Are Killing Your Business   13
- Retail Isn't the Only Victim   19
- Disruption Case Study #1: How Social Media Has Disrupted the PR Industry   19
- Disruption Case Study #2: Comfortable, Middle Class, Professional: There Is an App for That   21
- The Offline Advantage (Albeit Short-lived)   22

CHAPTER 2 – UNLIMITED STOCK   25
- Your Virtual Showroom   29
- Expert Advice: Q&As and Unbiased Customer Reviews   30
- How a Negative Comment Can Help Influence a Sale   31
- The Double Negative Review – A Good Thing   32

CHAPTER 3 – GOING MULTI-CHANNEL AND SELLING EVERYWHERE   35

    Multi-Channel Retail Case Study:
Tesco – Every Little Bit Helps   37
    Online Marketplaces - The Opportunity   41
    The Pareto Principle and Online Marketplaces   43
    eBay and Big Data   45
    Big Data Case Study: If the Shoe Fits   45
    But Isn't eBay a Little Cheap and Nasty?   46
    Why eBay's New Logo Is So Important   47
    6 Reasons Why You Need to Take
another Look at eBay and Amazon   50
    The Downside of Online Marketplaces   51
    Coping with the High Cost of Selling on Online Marketplaces   53
    Growth Strategies   55
    Going Global   57
    Online Resources for Marketplace Sellers   57
    Alternative Marketplaces   59

CHAPTER 4 - BUILDING YOUR OWN ONLINE EMPIRE   63

    Website Design: Keep It Simple and
Don't Try to Re-Invent the Wheel   63
    The Young Ones (The Wrong 'Uns)   65
    Build It and They Might Not Come   65
    Generating Traffic   66
    Taking the Location Out of Your URL   66
    Paid Search   67
    Email Marketing   69
    Social Media Marketing   69
    Content Marketing   70
    SEO   70
    Affiliate Marketing   71

CHAPTER 5 – WHEN BRICKS AND MORTAR HOLD YOU BACK — 73

- Is Your Warehouse/Stockroom an Asset or a Burden? — 73
- You Don't Make Money Stuffing Envelopes — 75
- The 4-Hour Work Week — 77
- 10 Productivity Hacks to Make Your Business More Efficient — 78
- A Simple Formula for Finding Happiness in Whatever You Do — 80
- Putting Customers' Happiness First — 81

CHAPTER 6 – CUSTOMER CARE — 83

- Try Before You Buy — 84
- Showrooming – How Real World Retailers Can Fight Back — 85
- The Price is Right — 86
- Big Box Retailers and Their Online Aliases — 88
- The Impact of Social Media on Customer Care and Your Reputation — 89
- Added Value Delivery Options Bolster Online Reputation — 90
- Why Fast and Free Is Not Always the Best Option — 91
- Click and Collect — 91
- The Future of Home Delivery — 92

CHAPTER 7 – CUSTOMER RETENTION - COME BACK SOON — 93

- Email Marketing — 94
- Some Basic Rules Regarding Email — 95
- A Tale of Two Bicycle Shops — 97

CHAPTER 8 – LET'S GET SOCIAL — 103
- Social Media and Return on Investment — 104
- 6 Places to Find Buried Treasure (ROI) on Social Media — 104
- Finding the Time to Get Social — 106
- Which Social Network is Right for Your Business? — 107
- Building an Audience on Social Media — 108
- 6 Tips to Build a Following on Social Media — 109
- Social Media's Role in Your Retention Strategy — 110
- Are You Asking Your Customers for Their Twitter Handles? — 110

CHAPTER 9 – ALTERNATIVE STREAMS OF REVENUE — 113
- Diversification – Big News — 113
- Flying a Different Route — 114
- Identifying New Revenue Generating Opportunities — 114
- Eating My Own Dog Food — 115
- Even the Big Guys Are Doing It — 115

CHAPTER 10 - BACK IN THE REAL WORLD — 117

ABOUT THE AUTHOR

John W. Hayes is a marketing strategist, public speaker and author who specialises in helping small and medium-sized businesses succeed in an environment which is increasingly influenced (and now more frequently disrupted) by the online economy.

In a career spanning more than 20 years, he has worked alongside some of the biggest names in eCommerce and online marketing including Amazon, Google and eBay while holding positions with technology companies such as ChannelAdvisor, iContact, Vocus (now Cision) and Viralheat. He has written for a wide range of print and online media including The Daily Mail, The Sun, The Yorkshire Post, Internet Retailing, The Marketer, eSellerMedia, Tamebay, Enterprise Nation and Everything PR.

His two previous books, *Becoming THE Expert: Enhancing Your Business Reputation through Thought Leadership Marketing* and *A Crash Course in Email Marketing for Small and Medium-sized Businesses* (both published by Brightword Publishing/ Harriman House) have topped the bestselling marketing and sales book charts on both sides of the Atlantic and continue to sell internationally.

He regularly delivers educational workshops, focusing on content, email and social media marketing for small and medium-sized businesses and often speaks at small business and marketing events across the United Kingdom, mainland Europe and the United States.

For more information and to receive occasional updates on his latest writing, events and other projects, you can follow John on Facebook: http://www.facebook.com/becomingtheexpert, Twitter: @john_w_hayes or subscribe to his email newsletter here: http://www.becomingtheexpert.com/subscribe.

PREFACE

If you work on the high street, you won't need reminding that traditional, bricks and mortar retail hasn't had an easy go of it in recent years. During turbulent economic times, barely a week went by without breaking news of another major high street multiple facing catastrophic failure. Sadly, the final death throes of the many small and independent retailers joining them in bankruptcy went largely unreported. It's a depressing thought, and one that not only impacts those who work in the industry but potentially damages the quality of life of each and every one of us, as our towns and city centres slowly come apart at the seams.

But there is light at the end of the tunnel and, as an eternal optimist, I'm pleased to start this book on a positive note.

After half a decade of financial gloom, it looks like the economy might just be turning a corner. At time of writing (October 2014), retail sales in the UK are on the up (increasing by 4.3 per cent since the previous year) and analysts are predicting bumper revenues in the run up to Christmas bolstered by high profile, US-style sales events like Black Friday and Cyber Monday.

Anecdotally, even on the streets of the northern English town where I live (one of the worst affected by the global downturn), I'm seeing wooden hoardings being pulled down from tired, old shop fronts and new businesses rising from the ashes of our once feared, soon-to-be derelict high streets. Perhaps it's a little early to be so optimistic (we'll know more by the time this book is printed) – but this sounds like good news for everyone.

But this doesn't necessarily mean a return to easy street.

Competition, complacency and the high costs associated with operating a "traditional" high street business all still represent a significant risk. However, for many businesses which continue to struggle on today's high streets, it is all too easy to point the finger of blame for their decline at factors, which they believe, are beyond their control.

The Internet, alongside the wider economy, out-of-town shopping and the major supermarkets, is a very obvious target when looking for a fall guy responsible for the decline of the retail industry in our inner cities and town centres. But is this fair?

According to the UK Office for National Statistics, in August 2014 the Internet accounted for only 11 per cent of all retail sales. There is no doubt the Internet represents a major challenge for the high street but it is not solely (or even significantly) to blame for its current difficulties.

Instead of looking to apportion blame, the question these businesses should be asking themselves is why should a high street business not move with the times and attempt to harness some of the amazing opportunities available to their high-tech counterparts?

I would personally argue that the Internet was not to blame for the demise of major high street chains like Woolworths or Comet who left our high streets and retail parks (in the UK) with gaping holes and shuttered retail units. In fact, I believe the Web could have offered both of these brands a significant lifeline, had they been more interested in competing in a digital age than defending a glorious past. It was complacency, poor management, a complete lack of agility (something that Internet brands definitely do not lack) and a general lack of direction that killed these high street behemoths. These were poor businesses living on borrowed time. The Internet and the weak economy simply put them out of their misery.

In the face of online competition some businesses will struggle more than others.

It could be argued that the Web disrupted the travel industry and forced the closure of numerous independent high street travel agents. Similarly, booksellers and record stores may also have fallen foul of mighty online retailers and changes in technology. But using the same argument, the Internet has also significantly disrupted the gaming/gambling industry with many bookmakers taking their businesses offshore and setting up online. Despite this, they continue to thrive on (and some would suggest are beginning to suffocate) the high street. Taking the ethical questions surrounding the gaming industry's grip on the high street out of the equation, I would suggest the difference between success and failure was their ability to identify new business trends, attract new customers, drive new streams of revenue and take advantage of opportunities as and when they arrive (like the sudden availability of prime retail space at knockdown prices). Both the downturn and technology (alongside some clever and arguably, aggressive marketing) have been good to the gambling industry.

Not all high street businesses can expect to survive in the digital age.

Others, however, will thrive and this includes the very best independent, customer-focused travel agents, booksellers and record stores. I believe these successful companies can enhance their fortunes by adopting business strategies normally associated with their online competitors. This doesn't mean they will simply transfer their business from a high street operation to an online enterprise (many will develop a more forward looking "clicks and mortar" business model). They will become more social, more customer-focused and more agile. In short, they will become better real world businesses.

> *I believe these successful companies can enhance their fortunes by adopting business strategies normally associated with their online competitors."*

WHO IS THIS BOOK FOR?

This book is for any entrepreneur, business owner or marketer who wants to future-proof their business, drive real world sales and maximise the potential of their traditional bricks and mortar operations using the techniques widely adopted by their online counterparts.

While many of the opportunities discussed in this book focus on the retail sector, they will be equally useful in the hospitality, entertainment or service industries.

This book will also prove beneficial for many small online businesses which have not yet harnessed some of the opportunities available to them via online marketing and customer retention techniques.

Many of the techniques discussed in this book will require some basic computer skills. I like to think if you can send an email or list an item for sale on an online auction site like eBay, you already possess many of the skills you will need to take advantage of many of the online opportunities available to you today.

Where more advanced techniques are covered, I have been careful to keep any jargon to a minimum as well as providing a list of useful resources where you can find additional support. Other strategies detailed on these pages will require little more than a little common sense, the adjustment of some basic business practices and the desire to make a change for the better.

Agility is key to succeeding as a traditional bricks and mortar business in the digital age. Now that business moves at the speed of the Internet, sitting back and delaying change is no longer an option. This book has been written to help you identify the first steps to developing an agile business strategy and start moving quickly and efficiently.

If there are any topics covered in this book you would like to discuss in more detail, please do not hesitate to contact me via Twitter: @john_w_hayes, Facebook: http://www.facebook.com/becomingtheexpert or Email: becomingtheexpert@gmail.com.

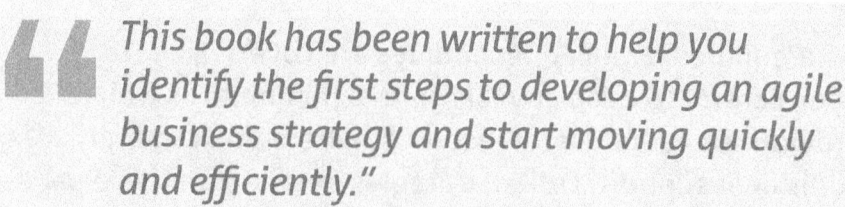

This book has been written to help you identify the first steps to developing an agile business strategy and start moving quickly and efficiently."

CHAPTER 1 – FIRST IMPRESSIONS COUNT

First impressions rarely count more than they do in the retail environment. Sadly, this is an area where many traditional retailers let themselves down, putting them at a massive disadvantage to their online contemporaries.

Walk down any high street and you will see a list of plain lazy retail mistakes that leave a bad taste in consumers' mouths and damage the reputation and allure of our inner cities and town centres.

Irregular opening hours, lackluster service, poor signage and tired window displays are all driving your customers online in droves. Factor in conditions outside of your control such as the weather or the cost of parking and you have a battle on your hands. A battle, many would have you believe, the Internet is winning.

To be forewarned is to be forearmed and so understanding the advantage online retailers have over the high street is key to winning back customers and keeping them coming back for good.

THE ONLINE ADVANTAGE

Selling online isn't as cheap or as easy as many high street businesses would believe. Despite the fact that many online retailers enjoy lower business rates and rents than their high street competitors, they do have to pay for the privilege of visitors landing on their website. Driving traffic via paid search networks, comparison shopping engines, Search Engine Optimisation (SEO) and email marketing, etc., to a website and maintaining customer loyalty online is an expensive business. Successful online retailers understand that this investment (and any profit it generates) can be lost in the brief second it takes a customer to click their mouse and visit another page. Even in the "low cost" online retail environment, a bad first impression can be an expensive mistake. Because of this, online retailers are rarely complacent about how their customers perceive their businesses, investing millions of pounds each year in usability, conversion and analytics (tracking people from the moment they enter a site until the moment they leave and even beyond).

When a customer lands on a website, what they see is often very different from the reality of the online operation's true situation.

A website's front end (the bit the consumer sees) is essentially just a glossy skin pulled tight over several pieces of clever technology bolted together (often very clumsily) to ensure as near a seamless shopping experience as possible. It is very easy to make even the cheapest web-based shopping technology look very professional. Behind the sleek exterior is a different story – but because nobody sees that, it doesn't really matter.

Nobody cares what an online retailer's warehouse looks like, where it is located and whether or not the warehouse team member picking and packing your purchases has had a good wash and shave that morning (or even that week).

Of the many online retailers' warehouses I have personally visited, very few of them fall into the multi-million pound, high-tech, temperature-controlled, county-sized facilities operated by the likes of Amazon. Most are freezing cold sheds, situated on less than salubrious industrial estates in the outer most corners of the UK. But this doesn't matter to the online customer who will never see this side of the business. No matter what state an online retailer's back room operations are in, it is very easy for them to throw up a highly professional, completely flexible façade to sell from behind.

When you shop online you don't see the warehouse manager sharing a crafty cigarette with the forklift driver in the car park or hear any unprofessional language coming from the man wearing the Hooters t-shirt (in my experience there is always a man in a Hooters t-shirt) while pulling items from the shelf and wrapping them in bubble wrap prior to dispatch. Online retail tends to be quite an anonymous business – this helps them keep costs down and maintain margins despite heavy discounting. In fact, online retail is so anonymous that many customers judge their service entirely on the quality of the courier (a third party business) who delivers their packages.

Online retailers have the advantage of being able to change the appearance of their virtual shop windows in a click. Sophisticated online retailers will even be able to match the appearance of their store to the individual customer's liking, based on previous purchases and engagements. Imagine being able to show a bespoke window display to everyone who passes your shop. This is what traditional retailers are up against – but it gets worse for the traditional retailer.

Finding any item online is seldom more arduous than a couple of clicks of a mouse. Online shoppers rarely enter an online shop via the front door (or home page). More often than not, they arrive from a quick search on a search engine like Google and land directly on the product or category page of the specific item they are interested in. On landing, the online shopper is then presented with a series of mechanisms deployed to help them make their decision and buy quickly. These mechanisms include compelling sales copy including detailed product descriptions (which can often include technical specifications that will shame even the most knowledgeable sales assistant), the promise of rapid, cheap or even free delivery, high resolution product images (which may even allow the viewer to rotate the image and zoom in to view any fine detail), independent product reviews and suggestions for further purchases.

Thanks to advances in eCommerce technology, even the smallest online retailers can offer their customers a really seamless experience, allowing them to search, find and purchase within a few clicks of a mouse (or increasingly a few taps on the screen of a tablet device or mobile phone).

When you take all of this into consideration, you'll understand why it is time to lift your game and start fighting back.

So, what does this mean for traditional retailers?

It means they always have to be at the top of their game. It means they need to get staffing levels right at busy times so customers are served promptly and professionally. It means sales assistants need to be trained and ready to help customers with difficult questions. It means window displays should always be enticing and changed regularly and signage is both clear and informative. It also means your premises need to be clean and bright and your shelves are always well stocked.

8 LAZY RETAIL MISTAKES THAT ARE KILLING YOUR BUSINESS

1. **Irregular Opening Hours:** With full-time jobs, children in and out of school and otherwise generally busy lives, you'll want to make it as easy as possible for your customers to visit your store. This means you need to be open and at your most efficient (meaning you have enough staff on hand to serve your customers in a timely, courteous and professional manner) at a time that suits your customers, not you or your employees. This might mean having extra staff available to cover lunch times, being open before and after the school run, in the late evenings, on weekends and public holidays. It also means the days of leaving a "Back in 15 Minutes" sign in the window when you nip out for a sandwich are over. Remember, a customer with limited time to spare will soon learn to avoid your shop if there is no guarantee it will be open. Smaller businesses with limited staff might want to close during slower trading periods. Very few customers will begrudge a small business closing on a Monday

or Tuesday afternoon if its opening hours are well publicised and stuck to rigidly.

2. **Poor Curb Appeal:** Bad lighting and/or poor window displays can completely destroy a retailer's reputation before a customer has even stepped foot into your premises. Having good curb appeal is not only important to passing motorists, who need to be made aware within just a few seconds that a shop is open, sells the kind of items they are looking for and persuades them to pull over and find a (potentially expensive) parking space. Your shop should also appear warm and inviting enough to persuade someone, perhaps already heavily laden down by shopping on a cold and wet day, to walk that extra 20 meters or cross that busy road to make their way to your door.

3. **Never Ending Sales:** All good things must come to an end and this includes your seemingly never-ending sale. There is nothing wrong with having a permanent sale rail to clear end-of-line stock but a permanent, all-encompassing sale will make you look cheap and make it difficult (if not impossible) to ever sell anything at full price again. It makes better business sense to be known as a retailer offering good value, great customer service and detailed product knowledge. Get this right and you might even be able to charge a premium for your goods.

4. **Too Much/Too Little Stock:** This can prove to be a bit of a balancing act. While the pile them high and sell them cheap strategy works for some businesses, it can also

dissuade customers from shopping at your store if they become overwhelmed by the sheer volume of stock. The opposite is also true in that too little stock can leave a shop looking empty and unloved or in the case of many high-end retailers, simply pretentious.

5. **The Apologetic Sale:** Have you ever heard yourself or a member of your staff commenting on or even apologising for the price of an item. Value is in the eye of the consumer and so you should never comment or apologise for the high price of an item. An apology insinuates that you believe your stock isn't worth the price tag displayed. Remember, good value doesn't always mean low prices.

6. **Surly Employees:** Do your staff look bored or underemployed? Are they moping around behind the counter and trying to avoid eye contact with your customers? Do they welcome your customers with indifference and make the place feel cold and unwelcoming? Worse still, do you or your employees greet your customers while huddled in a group, smoking cigarettes in your doorway, making your premises look untidy (and perhaps even dirty)? It might be time to have a quiet word with yourself and your employees and smarten yourselves up a little.

7. **Poor Product Knowledge:** Many people only hit the high street because they need a little advice. This is particularly true when making buying decisions for large or considered purchases like consumer

electronics, household electrical items or luxury goods. Sadly, many retailers (including many large high street names) let themselves down in this direction and fail to provide the kind of training (or incentives) their staff need to be able to offer the kind of support and advice your customers demand.

8. **Limited Payment Options:** I'm sorry, but in this day and age it is unacceptable not to accept payments via a wide range of credit or debit cards. Your customers shouldn't have to ask if you accept card payments. They should expect it. They should also expect that your staff know how to use the card payment machines before they are let loose on the shop floor.

The above problems might seem inconsequential to some retailers, but they can have severe repercussions for your business beyond causing a minor inconvenience for your customers. You should also bear in mind that these problems are rarely seen in the online environment. Once you lose a customer to an online brand it can be incredibly difficult (if not impossible) to win them back. If their experience is truly terrible, they will share it with their friends and family and may even spread the bad news even wider via social media (the modern, highly charged version of negative word-of-mouth marketing). Successful online retailers (who are not immune to criticism) understand the importance of creating a lasting impression and invest considerable time, effort and money to ensure an all-round positive experience.

What bad retail habits do you see in your business and how could you change them to ensure a brighter future for the high street?

Fixing one or two small problems can have a big impact on the future of your business. Unfortunately, some retailers might be beyond help. Sadly, when these businesses fold (and they inevitably always do), the scars they leave on our high streets impact everyone. Every high street is blighted with potential casualties. Take, for example, the following case study:

Retail Fail: On a recent trip to the historic city of York (home to a busy and eclectic retail environment), a friend asked if I would call into a particular shop and chase up an enquiry about a product she had made on the Internet several weeks earlier and which, despite several emails chasing the status of the enquiry, she had not heard anything back from the proprietor. Entering the shop, I was pleased to see it was brightly lit and the stock (mainly craft related items) well displayed - but something was definitely amiss. Actually, two things were definitely amiss. First and foremost, despite there being several customers in the shop, there didn't appear to be anyone actually working there. Secondly, none of the stock appeared to be priced. In the time it took me to find the store owner (hiding in a stock room), she had lost a handful of potential customers. I asked about my friend's order and was greeted with a blank stare, before she informed me that she didn't bother with her email very often. We were then interrupted by a customer enquiring how much a particular item was and her reply was staggering. She actually said,

"Oh, I don't know, between £10 and £20". The customer left the shop disappointed and slightly confused. I asked how business was and she complained about the cost of renting good retail space in York, while ignoring the phone ringing in the background. We left without making a purchase.

This might be an extreme case of how retailers are failing their customers on the high street but, hand-on-heart, consider how many times you have not followed up on a telephone call or been a little tardy in answering your emails. And while you would surely never consider displaying stock without first marking it up, we can all get a little lazy with our point of sale or the speed at which we engage customers in conversation at times.

Your customers deserve better treatment. They are savvy consumers with sophisticated tastes. If you are unable (or unwilling) to serve them in the manner they deserve and expect, they will go elsewhere.

Now consider how online brands manage their customer communication channels, employing email, telephone support, online chat and, increasingly, rapid response social media listening centres (where customers don't even have to make direct contact to be highlighted as a potential customer).

In this socially-enabled age, where everything moves quicker, lazy high street retailers will be punished.

RETAIL ISN'T THE ONLY VICTIM

I don't want you to develop a persecution complex and start thinking that as a retailer (or other high street business) you are a bit of a victim. The high street is not the only sector struggling in the digital age. If you think everyone else is having an easy time, think again.

DISRUPTION CASE STUDY #1: HOW SOCIAL MEDIA HAS DISRUPTED THE PR INDUSTRY

This abridged blog post first appeared on the ViralHeat blog (http://bit.ly/1FwwDY6):

> *As many of my former colleagues in the newspaper industry will attest, the mainstream news channels (print, broadcast and even Web-based) just aren't very good at breaking news anymore.*
>
> *Desk bound by budget cuts, journalists are forced to play catch up on social media where the news, more often than not, breaks, is disseminated and discussed. This represents a seismic shift in power. The traditional media no longer has a monopoly on news. It is the people who witness or even make the news who are now the media.*
>
> ***#wearethemedia***
>
> *If you are struggling with this concept, take a look at the television news or your favourite newspaper website and see how much content comes from mobile phone footage, Twitter, Facebook and YouTube.*

For an industry like PR which is very much built on relationships, this can be highly disruptive.

PR is often as much about keeping certain items out of the news and steering the conversation than winning column inches or TV coverage. Having a degree of influence over a handful of editors and newsrooms is one thing but being able to keep a lid on a story breaking on social media is altogether a different story.

The modern PR must now not only monitor and maintain relationships with the traditional media, they must also keep a watchful eye over the completely unregulated social media landscape and be ready to tackle sparks of negativity before they become raging flame wars.

Having the correct technology in place to monitor the social web, engage with an ever-connected public and analyse the impact of these conversations is no longer a luxury. It is a vital component of any complete PR strategy. Anything less is half-baked and represents a huge risk to the PRs and their clients' reputations.

Now consider the following nightmare scenario. We are all at risk.

DISRUPTION CASE STUDY #2: COMFORTABLE, MIDDLE CLASS, PROFESSIONAL: THERE IS AN APP FOR THAT

This abridged blog post first appeared on Business2Community (http://bit.ly/1tnkb72):

> *If you consider yourself to be a comfortable, middle-class, professional person, the following statement should fill you with dread: There is an app for that.*
>
> *You might be an accountant, a city planner, a social worker – in fact, it doesn't matter what you do, because you're about to be replaced. It's only a matter of time before some bright spark announces that there is an app for your job.*
>
> *Don't laugh – it's happened before, and it will happen again.*
>
> *Technology has disrupted numerous industries, including retail, travel, financial services, telecommunications, publishing – the list goes on. There is absolutely no reason to believe your position is immune to the rapid march of technology.*
>
> *Now that you accept this, there are two things you can do.*
>
> 1. *Bury your head in the sand and hope it won't happen to you before you hit retirement.*
>
> 2. *Educate yourself about the opportunities technology offers your business and position yourself ahead of the curve (or, at the very least, so you can ride the wave).*

A former newspaper colleague of mine once wisely proclaimed, "When everyone is terminally ill, there is no victory in being the last to die." The newspaper industry was already in decline, and these were the days before the widespread adoption of the Internet which decimated the industry. Perhaps he could see into the future.

I was lucky and found a position in online publishing when nobody else wanted one.

So what are the first steps you need to take toward future-proofing yourself against the incoming tide of technology set to disrupt your comfortable life?

First, start doing the things you've been meaning to do for years, like engaging with technologies that will give you a competitive edge (email, social media, etc.). Second, keep an open mind to what is around the next corner, and this means reading more.

How will you future-proof your profession?

Remember: *The greatest threat to your business is not changing.*

THE OFFLINE ADVANTAGE (ALBEIT SHORT-LIVED)

When it comes to the art of selling, I really believe in the basic business principle that people buy from people they like and are inspired to buy from people they identify with. Clearly, the real world retailer with their warm, friendly and welcoming staff and their community of active customers who are only too willing to promote your business with a little positive word-of-mouth marketing has a huge advantage over their cold, faceless online competitors.

I'm obviously making a bit of an assumption here by believing all your staff to be warm, friendly and welcoming. However, if they are not, your customers will undoubtedly prefer the cold, faceless (but thoroughly efficient) online experience. I'm also assuming any word-of-mouth around your business is always positive.

You would however be naïve if you didn't think your online competitors had an ace up their sleeve when it comes to becoming more likeable. They do this by harnessing the power of their online communities of customers and browsers who provide them with human engagement in the form of online reviews, Q&As, Facebook "likes" and other social media shares. These communities are made up of people with a lot in common with you and your customers and, as such, are incredibly likeable.

All the major online brands are using this humanising technique and becoming more likable. This might explain why a company like Amazon has more than 25.8 million "likes" on Facebook. People "like" Amazon so much they want them to include them in their social lives.

CHAPTER 2 – UNLIMITED STOCK

Unlimited stock (or at the very least the perception of unlimited stock) is another area where the online retailer has a clear advantage over their bricks and mortar contemporaries.

When you select and buy a product online, you have no idea whether the retailer actually has that item in stock or not. It might be sitting in their warehouse, ready to be picked and packed. Alternatively, it might still be with the manufacturer or distributor, sitting in a third-party distribution network's warehouse or even with another online retailer ready to be drop shipped. There is even the possibility that it might not even exist yet with a growing number of products bought online (including books, CDs, DVDs, laptop computers and even cars) made on-demand.

Although most online retailers will hold some stock, their long-tail items (the items that perhaps don't sell so frequently, but allow them to maintain a complete catalogue of products) will often only be stored as data in their eCommerce management systems.

This gives the online retailer a considerable financial advantage of not having to pay for stock (which may lose value on a retailer's shelves) until an order is actually received and paid for.

When an order is received for an item not held in stock, the retailer's technology kicks in, locates the item and it is promptly dispatched, arriving with little evidence of the route it has taken from initial order to the customer's address.

This system of drop shipping and third-party fulfilment means even the smallest online retailer can appear to stock many thousands of product lines or SKUs (Stock Keeping Units). For example, a traditional book store might be able to stock upwards of 30,000 titles, whereas an online retailer could purport to sell millions. Similarly, an automotive spares and accessories retailer couldn't hope to stock components for every make and model of vehicle available, whereas an online retailer could present a more complete inventory. You can repeat this scenario over countless industry verticals.

While unlimited stock might seem an unsurmountable problem for the traditional retail operation, there are numerous opportunities to do a better job and compete with the online world.

Traditional retailers can, of course, order items not held in stock for customers but unlike the online retailer, they are unable to set the perception that they simply stock everything. If an item is not immediately available, the customer is much more likely to simply visit another shop or just go online. Because of this you need to change your customers' perception of how you handle stock.

Retail Fail: My eldest daughter asked for a violin for her seventh birthday. As parents with little musical experience beyond the occasional bout of air guitar when nobody is looking, we needed some advice. We visited a local, independent shop which we believed had a good reputation and made enquiries. We were told by a helpful assistant that she would need a half-sized instrument, but unfortunately they didn't have any in stock. We asked when they might be back in stock and the reply was, at very best, vague. In short, they didn't have a clue. We thanked the assistant for his help, went home and ordered the exact make and model as recommended by the shop assistant online and it was promptly delivered the next day.

Update: Some weeks later the very same music store was profiled in a local newspaper where the owner (an accountant) talked about his business which had been set up by his father (a musician) some 30 years previously. In the article, he boasted about having absolutely zero musical ability and little interest in the products he sold other than their profit margins. We initially visited his store because we believed he was an expert. We'll never visit again. **#PRFail**

Retail Fail: When it comes to large ticket purchases, my partner is very much still a big fan of the high street. So when our old dishwasher died, she insisted we spend the best part of the day visiting countless appliance stores looking for what should have been a fairly simple purchase. We wanted an integrated dishwasher (meaning the appliance could be disguised as a kitchen unit). Apparently, these units are not as fashionable as they used to be (what can I say, we are dinosaurs). Not one of the retailers we visited had them in stock. One of the independent retailers we visited was able to order one, but it was out of our price range. Another couldn't guarantee when it would be delivered (we don't like washing dishes in our house and need one ASAP). The independents' service however, was a dream compared to the big box retailers. They just said there was little demand for that kind of dishwasher and tried to sell us an item we didn't want. We headed home and within 20 minutes found and ordered an integrated dishwasher with speedy delivery at a price we considered fair. The frustrating thing was, we ended up purchasing this item via the online store of one of the retailers we had visited earlier in the day. That retailer was Comet – who famously fell into administration and closed its doors just before Christmas in 2012, blaming, amongst other things, competition from the Internet for their demise. Despite winning our custom, because we visited their site via an advert on Google (which we clicked on several times during our online search), they probably didn't see the kind of profits they could have achieved if they had been more helpful in their retail store.

Retailers need to stop telling people that they don't hold particular items in stock. Instead, try offering them the type of service the online retailer offers as standard. Tell them the item is on order, take the payment and, for the sake of convenience, deliver it directly to their home address at no extra cost to the customer. Whenever possible include a promotion (this doesn't have to be a discount voucher) for their next in-store purchase to maximise their chance of return.

The cost of delivery might eat into your profits, but this high-level of service should ensure something that online retailers never take for granted – repeat business increasing customer lifetime value. Customer retention is discussed in detail in chapter seven of this book.

YOUR VIRTUAL SHOWROOM

No matter how big your retail premises, you will always be limited in terms of stock when compared to your online competitors. This means you have to start getting smart about how you demonstrate you have access to the same "complete" range of products.

This has to go beyond stocking a range of print catalogues or having access to a manufacturer's database of products. Your customers need to know that you can get your hands on anything they can find on the Internet. This means having point-of-sale signage advising your customers that just because it is not on the shop floor doesn't mean it cannot be ordered. This also means training your staff to offer this service. Forward thinking retailers are arming their sales advisors with tablet computers (like the ubiquitous Apple iPad), enabling them to aid customers in their product search and secure orders which can be attributed to a specific store. In the future, many large bricks and mortar retailers might see their high street businesses as more of a marketing opportunity than a place to hold and sell stock.

Tip: Amazon can actually help your small retail business with flexible warehousing and shipping services. We'll talk more about this in chapter five of this book.

The Online Advantage: Online retailer Amazon enhances its vast catalogue of products (can you remember when they just sold books?) with an increasingly large selection of items from third party sellers. This means they can get their hands on virtually any product (including products that serve niche marketplaces and could perhaps be described as long tail sales opportunities) without having to invest in stock or warehousing. Due to the incredible range of products available from their virtual shelves, Amazon is very often the first place I will look when considering any purchase. If Amazon doesn't stock (or sell) an item, it probably doesn't exist. Because Amazon attracts millions of shoppers every single day, competition is fierce amongst its marketplace sellers to feature their products on their pages. This keeps prices low and, it could be argued, makes life even more difficult for the high street. Low costs do not impact Amazon's profitability because they take a percentage of every sale made via their marketplace and therefore can find profit in any sale regardless of available margin. Adding to this threat, a number of other large retailers such as Tesco and Argos in the UK and Walmart and Sears in the US are also building their own third party marketplaces.

There are of course many opportunities (and many hidden threats) for retailers hoping to take advantage of these retail giants' third party marketplaces – which we will uncover in the following chapter.

EXPERT ADVICE: Q&AS AND UNBIASED CUSTOMER REVIEWS

Many people choose to visit the high street because they believe they will receive exceptional advice based on years of experience and detailed product knowledge. Despite this, my experience at many retailers (especially the big box variety) has been abysmal.

Note: Unless you provide your sales staff with the resources they need to become more informed, proactive sales professionals, you are letting your employees, your customers and, ultimately, your business down.

You probably won't be surprised to learn that, yet again, the online retailer has a massive advantage here over their high street counterpart. Despite not having frontline sales staff, the online retailer has the ability to advise and inform, allowing their customers to make an informed choice. They do this by harnessing the power of their online communities and featuring detailed product reviews (from experts and consumers) and carefully considered Q&As alongside their product descriptions.

Remember: Real world businesses are increasingly coming under the scrutiny of online reviews. A series of positive or negative reviews on a site like TripAdvisor (http://www.tripadvisor.co.uk) can make or break a hotel's or restaurant's reputation. Even the humble tradesman (builders, plumbers, electricians, etc.) are being reviewed online via sites like Checkatrade (http://www.checkatrade.com). We all have to step up our game if we are going to shine in the digital age.

HOW A NEGATIVE COMMENT CAN HELP INFLUENCE A SALE

It may, however, surprise you to learn that negative, as well as positive customer reviews can help sell a product or service.

I spend a lot of time reading customer reviews, particularly when making large purchases. I'm not only looking for positive comments. Sometimes even the most negative comments can help me make a positive buying decision.

Booking the annual family summer holiday is a great example of a time when I actively seek out what I call double negative reviews. A standard negative review might suggest a hotel is dirty or the staff unfriendly. However, a double negative review could actually be a positive review.

Let me explain.

With two young children, I'm looking for something reasonably priced (although there is always a degree of flexibility here when my partner gets involved), with great facilities for the kids (good pool, children's club, etc.), good food, close enough to the action (good restaurants, beaches, etc.), without being too rowdy. In short, if I am well-fed and can find a bit of peace and quiet to read a good book while the kids are occupied, I'm happy. More often than not it is the double negative reviews that sell the trip for me.

THE DOUBLE NEGATIVE REVIEW – A GOOD THING

A double negative for me is a complaint that the hotel does not cater to teenagers or the rowdy 18-30 crowd. Another double negative might complain that the food is "foreign" as opposed to "British". In fact, if any review complains that a hotel appears to cater more to German or French tourists (who demand more for their money than many British tourists), that's another plus point. The fact that I don't speak German or French means that even if the hotel's clientele are unhappy or have found something to complain about their holiday, unless I'm directly affected, I remain blissfully ignorant and ultimately, happy.

This principle of the double negative review also works in the world of retail. For example, a retailer selling mobile phones might publish a review of a device complaining that a basic model might not boast a high quality camera or lack certain functionality. This seemingly negative review could actually be seen as positive for someone buying a phone for an elderly relative (perhaps providing them with a vital lifeline while retaining independent living), where ease of use will often outweigh functionality.

> *A standard negative review might suggest a hotel is dirty or the staff unfriendly. However, a double negative review could actually be a positive review."*

CHAPTER 3 – GOING MULTI-CHANNEL AND SELLING EVERYWHERE

Too many bricks and mortar retailers restrict themselves in terms of geography and time. There is, with a few exceptions, no such thing as a local online retailer. When a product is listed online it is available (very often globally) in a 24/7/365 trading environment.

In the digital age, your customers want to choose when and where they shop. This could be on the high street, on your website, via a mobile phone or a third-party marketplace like Amazon or eBay. Savvy retailers understand this and enable their customers to find them no matter how they prefer to shop.

This means branching out into the world of eCommerce and competing with the online retailers in their own backyard. Yes, I'm telling you to take your beloved, traditional, bricks and mortar business and put it online.

For the more technically challenged amongst you, this need not be as challenging as it might seem at first. I'm convinced if you can send an email, update a Facebook status or book a holiday online – you already have the skills to sell online.

Note: It might seem counterintuitive to suggest to a real world retailer that they should take the battle against the online retailers online, especially when they are trying to focus on protecting their high street business, but consider the following. If you have taken a long, hard look at your retail business and believe you have done everything you can to attract, retain and maximise the returns from your existing and potential customers, where else can you go? Are you going to slowly lose market share to the Web before slowly and painfully going out of business? Are you going to expand your high street business into other premises at great expense, increasing your risk and adding to your management woes of hiring, training and learning to trust new staff? Or are you going to maximise your returns with your existing infrastructure and staff? I know what I would rather do. Selling the concept of going online to your business partners and colleagues should be a fairly easy process if you are reducing risk, enhancing your traditional business and protecting everyone involved in the business' future.

Remember: It is possible to offer your customers all the benefits of a local business (personal service, expert advice, etc.) while extending your reach via the Internet. In addition to increasing your business' reach, an online presence will also drive sales from people within your local community who perhaps cannot shop at your physical shop due to work or personal commitments (these could include factors such as age or disability). There is also the sheer convenience factor of shopping online. British supermarket Tesco provides a great example of this convenience factor as they do an amazing job serving local communities with their online service offering home delivery and click and collect services. Below, we'll look at how your business (no matter how big or small) can adopt strategies from this supermarket giant to ensure profitability and growth.

MULTI-CHANNEL RETAIL CASE STUDY: TESCO – EVERY LITTLE BIT HELPS

Tesco might have a bad reputation in the world of independent retailing (matched more recently in the world of accountancy best practice), but in terms of multi-channel retail their business is almost perfect.

There are very few towns or cities in the UK that have not felt the impact Britain's biggest retailer has had on their high streets. However, it amuses me that some of the people most vocal in their criticism of the Tesco brand can often be found filling their shopping baskets at the supermarket's tills each week. Some might suggest they have no choice but to shop there. However, in the town where I live there are still two very busy markets selling a wide range of competitively priced fresh meat, fish, fruit and vegetables, alongside numerous other independent retailers which could supply many of the products we buy weekly from the supermarket. Make no mistake, we don't buy from Tesco because we have no choice. We buy from Tesco because it is convenient.

Even before the advent of online grocery shopping, the likes of Tesco trumped the high street in terms of parking convenience (perhaps car ownership has had bigger impact on high street sales than proliferation of the major supermarkets), choice and price (although my local "traditional" market tends to be cheaper). The Internet has simply super-charged this level of convenience and is a huge area of growth and profits for many supermarket brands.

Luckily, I believe even the smallest retailers can learn from the Tesco experience and adopt some of their strategies to future-proof their businesses.

Tesco's core grocery business reaches its customers via three main routes.

1. **Traditional Retail:** Where customers visit their premises to select and pay for products personally.

2. **Home Delivery:** Goods are purchased online, picked by employees from a local store's shelves and delivered at a specific time by a local delivery team.

3. **Click and Collect:** Goods are selected online, picked from shelves in exactly the same way as the home delivery service and then stored onsite for collection.

The beauty about all three of these models is they largely utilise existing store infrastructure with no need for additional warehousing or fulfilment centres (although the supermarket has opened "dark" stores in highly-populated areas with the sole purpose of fulfilling online orders). All stock, whether selected by a customer or picked by an employee to fulfil an online order, is managed in exactly the same way prior to purchase. Staff employed to fulfil online orders can be deployed to other areas of the business depending on demand. And let's face it, home delivery is hardly a new concept in retail, although for many of us, the days of the local butcher delivering meat by bike seem like ancient history now.

But Tesco goes further and in recent years has launched a third-party online marketplace, helping it compete with the likes of Amazon and eBay and offer a wider range of products. Tesco's online marketplace is made up of carefully selected retail partners guaranteeing high levels of service and expanding their available product range from garden plants to musical instruments, alongside other items not normally stocked by the supermarket brand.

Due to the physical size of Tesco's network of stores and the sheer number of products they stock, they of course employ highly sophisticated eCommerce systems to manage their online operation alongside a fleet of delivery vehicles and a large number of dedicated staff. This is not a low-cost operation, but it is easy to see how when scaled back to suit a small, independent retailer this model could easily and cost-effectively be adopted using off-the-shelf, affordable software and existing infrastructure.

Tip: Home delivery used to be the norm for small independent retailers. Could your customers be persuaded to buy more, or perhaps bigger, bulkier items, if they knew they didn't have to carry them home on public transport or hump bags around countless other shops?

Note: Since writing this chapter, Tesco itself has suffered considerably with a dramatic decline in profits and share price and considerable damage to its reputation following bad press resulting from poor accounting practice (hot on the heels of the horse meat scandal of 2013). This just goes to show that even the big boys are not immune to competition, incompetence and the failure to understand what their customers actually want.

Taking Your First Steps into the World of Multi-Channel Online Retail

Taking your first steps into the world of multi-channel retail need not be a daunting task. In fact it could be as simple as listing a few items on an online marketplace like eBay or Amazon.

Online marketplaces allow retailers to explore a number of options:

1. **Distressed Inventory:** Stock left sitting on your shelves takes up valuable space, prevents you from re-investing in your retail business and costs you money. eBay and Amazon provide the perfect opportunity to shift distressed inventory (end-of-line, last season, returns, etc.) and release valuable capital back into your business.

2. **Supplementary Income:** Online marketplaces allow retailers to dip their toes in and out of the world of eCommerce, adjusting the flow of trade to suit their business needs. For example, a retail store in a popular tourist resort might want to increase sales outside of its peak summer sales period, but turn off online sales when the holiday crowds return. This could help your business retain staff throughout the year and maximise your profit earning potential.

3. **Click and Collect:** Not all online sales need to be shipped to your customers. eBay provides the perfect

opportunity to attract people to your bricks and mortar store to collect their purchases providing you with the perfect up-sell opportunity.

4. **Out-of-Hours Service:** Not all of your customers will be able to visit your store during regular opening hours. Promoting an online store to your local community will enable you to reach potential customers who would normally have no other choice than to visit major online shopping brands.

5. **Clicks and Mortar:** More and more businesses are blurring the lines between on and offline. Why limit yourself to just being on the high street or online when it is perfectly possible to do both?

6. **Pure Play Online Retail:** If you cannot beat them, join them. Some high street retailers, particularly those who sell to more niche markets where local customers might be limited, have evolved into pure play online retailers. This means their bricks and mortar stores are little more than showrooms (often retained for the benefit of suppliers, many of which prefer to deal purely with real world retail stores).

ONLINE MARKETPLACES - THE OPPORTUNITY

You should not underestimate the opportunity available to retailers via online marketplaces. In the UK, eBay alone hosts more than 200,000 professional sellers turning over an estimated £6bn in sales each year.

The online marketplaces represent a significant opportunity to not only test the waters and learn more about the art of selling online, but also to build a significant Internet-based business without requiring too much technical knowledge or any design skills. For example, many products can be added to Amazon by simply clicking the "Sell on Amazon" button found on most product pages and then filling out a simple form regarding price, condition and delivery options. Amazon takes care of credit card payments, delivery costs (crediting your account with a set amount to cover postage) and sends the money for any orders received directly to your bank account. Listing products on eBay is almost as easy, although you will need a PayPal account to handle payments which are made directly to you.

While eBay and Amazon represent a great starting point for any business taking their first steps online, both sites demand a great deal in terms of customer service from their sellers. Orders need to be processed and dispatched quickly and professionally. eBay businesses live and die on the feedback they receive from their customers and in these days of next day delivery and free returns, even the most aggressive bargain hunters on eBay expect great service. Be ready to answer a lot of questions from customers prior to dispatch and pray the weather or industrial action doesn't cause any reputation busting delays with your goods getting to their final destination. Similarly, Amazon does not take prisoners and the algorithms (a mathematical formula executed by a computer) they employ to police their service will shut down poor performers without question and extremely limited recourse. Because of this, it is best to start with kid steps and build up slowly.

Starting slowly means building your multi-channel strategy one channel and a few products at a time. It is also advisable to start serving your domestic market first before expanding out into international territories. Taking things easy will also help you find the correct balance between managing your online and your traditional bricks and mortar business, helping you analyse new opportunities and make adjustments to your business accordingly. Developing a new multi-channel strategy is very much a marathon and not a sprint. And just like in the world of sports, first time marathon runners need to put in the hours training first before building up gradually to their full distance.

THE PARETO PRINCIPLE AND ONLINE MARKETPLACES

For many retailers, having as wide a range of products available is important. Perhaps they believe the more expansive their inventory, the more you will sell. Perhaps they are wrong.

Although it might seem counterintuitive, for retailers looking to ramp up their online sales significantly it might not be the best approach to simply try to pile up as many products as possible and then attempt to effectively market everything you have on your shelves.

Too much choice can confuse consumers and may hinder them from making an informed buying decision. The longer a customer delays purchasing an item, the less chance they will have of actually buying your products. Too much choice may also confuse your marketing strategy as you attempt to spread limited marketing resources across a range of products, resulting in nothing getting the attention they deserve.

Regardless of how you market your products, there will always be a cost associated with targeting your audience (in terms of time and money). Some products might not have enough margin in them to justify high marketing costs. Others, particularly heavy or bulky items, even when successfully marketed might just be a logistic nightmare to sell and ship. Nightmares tend to be expensive.

Remember, slow moving products will tie up your capital and cost you money as they depreciate on your shelves, preventing you from re-investing in your business and maximising your profit earning potential.

The Pareto Principle (often referred to as the 80/20 rule) is a good rule of thumb when identifying the products you might want to market and sell. The Pareto Principle dictates that 80% of your turnover will come from 20% of your products. Conversely, this means that 80% of your products could actually cost you money and cause headaches for your business.

Therefore, identifying the 20% of products that will deliver 80% of your revenues (and more importantly profits), and cutting out the dead wood are key to successful online selling. In online retail, less could actually mean more.

EBAY AND BIG DATA

Big business is big on big data. This essentially means many big retailers spend a lot of time, money and resources analysing all available data on how and when their customers shop with them allowing them to make more informed strategic decisions. Loyalty programmes like Tesco's Club Card are essentially exercises in big data, allowing the retailer to understand who buys what and when. Cross referencing personal data with seasonal trends and even the weather forecast allows them to keep their shelves stocked with the right products at the right time.

But big data isn't only available to big business. Online tools like Terapeak (http://www.terapeak.com) allow even the humblest of eBay sellers to understand how products sell and at what price via the online marketplace. I have personally worked with online sellers who have used the data provided by Terapeak to completely inform their product strategy.

BIG DATA CASE STUDY: IF THE SHOE FITS

Kelly thought her life was all mapped out and running smoothly. She had always been career-minded and highly driven, successfully climbing the corporate ladder until she suddenly took ill and was hospitalised with a life threatening condition. Her priorities changed overnight. Ever resourceful, she used her lengthy recovery period to start planning for a very different future. The cut and thrust of life in the corporate world no longer appealed to her and so she quit her job (as well as abandoning a lifelong dream of starting a new life in

Australia) so she could stay close to the friends and family who supported her whilst ill. She knew she would still have to work to pay the bills and support her family, but she wanted to do so on her own terms. Setting up an eBay business seemed the ideal option. The only problem was, she had no experience in retail and didn't know what to sell.

Kelly's first investment was in technology. She subscribed to Terapeak and spent a month analysing what sold well (looking at volume, sales price, competition, etc.) via the online marketplace. Equipped with a shortlist of hot eBay products, she was then able to seek out suppliers armed with all the data she needed to make sure that she could buy stock that could be turned over quickly and return a healthy profit.

While Kelly is a self-confessed "shoeaholic", it was big data that helped her become one of the UK's largest shoe sellers on eBay and not her desire to surround herself with beautiful footwear. Sticking to her rule of keeping friends and family close, she now employs her husband, sister and their two children in the business.

BUT ISN'T EBAY A LITTLE CHEAP AND NASTY?

I come across this question (more often presented as a statement) all the time from retailers who perhaps feel eBay does not reflect the best image for their business. My answer is simple. Take a good look at the big name retailers currently trading on eBay. If eBay is good enough for retailers like House of Fraser, Superdry, Argos, Littlewoods, Tesco or Vodafone, who all actively sell on the marketplace, it's probably good enough for you.

In recent years eBay has done much to distance itself from its cheap and cheerful flea market image of old including a major re-branding exercise in 2012 which I wrote about in the following blog post which first appeared on the Business2Communty website (http://bit.ly/1Bnezmp).

WHY EBAY'S NEW LOGO IS SO IMPORTANT

When any multi-national organisation announces an attempt to refresh their image, perhaps a tweaking of their company logo or an adjustment in the hue of their corporate palate, it's normally met with derision from the general public.

How much is all this costing? What was wrong with the old identity? Does anyone care?

History is littered with costly rebranding mistakes. From British Airways' bid to remove the British flag from their aircraft's livery to Gap's short lived attempt to think outside of the box, the costs of rebranding have often exceeded replacing the office stationery and in some cases have caused long term damage to the brands.

But in eBay's case, I believe the redesign is fully justified.

eBay has lived with their quirky, jumbled up, colourful, old logo for the past 17 years. It has represented the brand well and has become one of the most recognised and loved corporate identifiers globally. The logo told you that eBay was fun and cheap and a little bit all over the place. It also helped cement eBay's appeal as a company built on a strong set of ideals and a community spirit (where anyone could trade).

The fact that many of eBay's customers feel so connected to the company makes it a very difficult proposition to rebrand. Some commentators have even suggested that eBay's President, Devin Wenig, has shown a degree of disrespect to the people who built the eBay community (the original eBay auction buyers and sellers) by announcing alongside the new logo: "This is the new eBay".

I disagree.

In recent years eBay has changed. But it has also stayed the same.

It still offers a profitable venue for individuals to list second hand and collectable items for sale either at auction or at a fixed price. It still offers businesses of all sizes the opportunity to sell end-of-line or distressed inventory that would otherwise be left sitting on warehouse shelves. And yes, it is increasingly becoming a channel of choice for big name retailers to list and sell brand new, full price items.

It is perhaps this third group of sellers that eBay is trying to appeal to the most with their new, clean, corporate logo. To these sellers, eBay's branding and positioning are incredibly important. While it might seem crazy to discount the idea of selling on such a high-traffic site as eBay because of their cheap and cheerful image, you have to remember that many big brand retailers see eCommerce with the same blinkered vision as they view the high street where image and positioning are still number one priorities. If eBay wants to attract big name retailers, it is eBay who has to be willing to change.

But I believe the benefits of big name sellers joining the ranks on eBay will be felt throughout the community as they attract more buyers to the site (who perhaps would never have thought of eBay in the past).

I'm not saying that this will make life easier for all sellers on eBay, some of who will see the arrival of more big brands on the site as a massive threat. But others will see the opportunity, perhaps diversify their range and offers (perhaps even improving their own brand identity) and continue to make a significant impact via eBay. I believe agility is the most significant factor in finding success in an online venture and this is one area where small sellers can wipe the floor with the big guys.

eBay's new logo symbolises their new position in the eCommerce environment. We should no longer think of eBay as a flea market on the Old Kent Road. Nor should we think of it as a department store on Oxford Street. It's somewhere in the middle, where big brands and local traders compete and thrive right next to each other. Perhaps it is closer to the high street shopping experience many of us wish we still had.

6 REASONS WHY YOU NEED TO TAKE ANOTHER LOOK AT EBAY AND AMAZON

If you need more persuasion to consider listing your products on eBay or Amazon, check out the following points:

1. **Traffic:** Not only are online marketplaces incredibly heavily trafficked (meaning they get a lot of visitors). As premier online shopping destinations they can guarantee a high percentage of visitors will be very much in a buying frame of mind when they land on your product pages and be keen to spend their money with you.

2. **Low Risk:** The cost of listing stock items on eBay is minimal and is actually free on Amazon. Seller fees only kick in once you have sold an item. Compare this to most other forms of acquisition marketing (print, broadcast and most other forms of online marketing) where all the costs are upfront, regardless of success.

3. **Customer Trust:** Both eBay and Amazon provide a secure, safe environment to conduct business and regularly police their retailers to ensure they stick to the rules and ensure that their customers (your customers) feel safe and secure when buying products via their marketplaces.

4. **Customer Acquisition:** eBay and Amazon provide a highly visible venue to acquire new customers and then drive them back to your own website (or even bricks and mortar store) through branding, packaging and a positive customer experience.

5. **Simple Technology:** Selling online can be daunting for many real world retailers. Thankfully, getting started with eBay and Amazon is incredibly simple (even for the most technophobic out there). As you advance (and become more confident) on the marketplaces there are a number of more sophisticated technology tools at your disposal which will take your marketplace business to the next level.

6. **You'll Be in Good Company:** With brands like Argos, House of Fraser, Tesco, Superdry and Vodafone selling on online marketplaces, you'll definitely be in good company.

THE DOWNSIDE OF ONLINE MARKETPLACES

While eBay and Amazon might offer a quick and easy method for aspiring online retailers to start selling their products online, there is also a downside. The two most common complaints I hear from online marketplace sellers are cost and competition.

While it can be very cheap (or even free) to list your products on online marketplaces, the cost of selling can actually be quite expensive. At the time of writing, Amazon UK charges a referral fee of anywhere between 8.05% on sales of large kitchen appliances to 28.75% for jewellery and a massive 40.25% for Kindle (reading devices) accessories. It should be remembered, online marketplaces are pure acquisition marketing channels. As anyone who has been in business for any length of time will tell you, acquiring new customers is expensive. The major problem many retailers face when selling via online marketplaces is they must pay the same expensive acquisition marketing costs each and every time someone buys from a listing, regardless of whether they are a repeat customer or not. Terms and conditions prevent retailers from re-marketing (using more cost efficient marketing channels like email marketing) to customers acquired via online marketplace sales.

Note: I talk in-depth about how online marketplace sellers can circumnavigate the issue of not being allowed to re-market to their customers via email in my book: *A Crash Course in Email Marketing for Small and Medium-sized Businesses.*

Before you start selling online, you need to fully understand your costs. These will initially include listing fees, final sales fees, postage and packaging costs and payment processing fees. These fees have a habit of adding up and can quickly destroy any margin you might have in a product. I meet countless online sellers every year who despite generating incredible growth in terms of turnover, see very little in the way of profits. I refer to these retailers as "busy fools", many of whom are too busy to see they are actually losing money. The moral of this story is equally valid on the high street as it is online: **Know your costs.**

Low (almost non-existent) barriers to entry mean competition is fierce across the online marketplace landscape. Unless you have access to a unique product, you will find competitors beating down your prices and putting, at times, incredible pressure on your margins. Many retailers on Amazon (who unlike eBay are also a retailer) feel the marketplace itself competes unfairly with their third-party sellers. There is no easy solution to this problem other than a little tough love. I've already stated in this book that agility is the key to surviving in business. Businesses that sit still and make little attempt to diversify their product ranges will struggle in the online world as much (and perhaps more so) than on the high street. Remember: **Stay agile.**

COPING WITH THE HIGH COST OF SELLING ON ONLINE MARKETPLACES

To counterbalance a high cost of sale, there are a number of strategies a retailer can adopt to protect their margin and retain profits.

1. **Diversify Your Product Range:** Diversifying your product range will reduce your risk of absolute failure when the bottom drops out of a particular line of products (and every product has a finite lifespan). Because online retail is an incredibly fast moving environment, sitting on the same products is a very risky business.

2. **Go Multi-Channel:** Set up shop across multiple online marketplaces (and if possible geographic territories – both eBay and Amazon operate global businesses, giving you the opportunity to sell internationally) before trying to move your customers over to your own website. In a perfect world, you'll want to drive the majority of your sales via your own site and cut out online marketplace seller's fees altogether (although the problem of driving traffic to your own site can represent a significant challenge).

3. **Embrace Technology:** Software like ChannelAdvisor, eSeller Pro and SellerExpress (more about them later in this chapter) can help you automate many of the time consuming processes (listing, re-listing, re-pricing, invoicing, creating packing and picking documents, etc.) involved with selling via online marketplaces. There are also a number for scalable and highly affordable eCommerce platforms (highlighted in chapter 4) which can help you quickly and easily develop your own online retail store and reduce your reliance on expensive marketplace channels. Technology will help you become a more efficient seller while freeing up your time so you can concentrate on more important tasks to build your business.

4. **Acquire and Retain:** Each and every time you sell a product on eBay or Amazon you are paying expensive acquisition rates even if they are a loyal, repeat customer. Careful branding and great customer service will enable you to drive customers to your own website where you can target them via targeted email marketing campaigns that can drive repeat purchases and increase Customer Lifetime Value (CLV).

5. **Cut Costs:** Always try and squeeze your suppliers for the best possible deal. A small saving on packaging materials or your standard delivery rate can make a big difference to your profits at the end of the year. Software solutions like MetaPack (http://www.metapack.com) can help you find the most efficient

delivery solutions, giving you a competitive edge. Remember, it is not only the available margin in a product that determines your profits.

6. **Outsource Your Warehouse Operations:** Services like Fulfilment by Amazon (FBA) can help you seamlessly scale up or down your online selling operation according to demand.

7. **Stay Savvy:** Watch the market. Alter your prices in line with your competition (up or down depending on demand) and don't be afraid to withdraw from a particular product line or marketplace if and when they become untenable.

GROWTH STRATEGIES

Managing a handful of listings on a single online marketplace can be a fairly easy process, but in order to truly maximise your potential you will want to dramatically increase the number of products available and develop a true multi-channel strategy across multiple sites and geographies. This can present a number of problems in terms of stock control and time management. This is where technology comes in. The good news is, thanks to the Internet, truly scalable and incredibly powerful online software solutions (often referred to as Software-as-a-Service or SaaS) used by major retail names are now available to much smaller businesses.

eCommerce sales management software provided by the likes of ChannelAdvisor (http://www.channeladvisor.com), eSellerPro (http://www.esellerpro.com), Linnworks (http://www.linnworks.com) and SellerExpress (http://www.sellerexpress.com) will help you manage your listings more efficiently across multiple marketplaces.

Technology automates many time consuming activities such as listing and re-listing products, managing stock levels over multiple channels, preventing overselling (which can place your online reputation at risk), managing your email communications regarding order confirmation and delivery notifications, and pricing strategies (ensuring your products are listed competitively and profitably), as well as providing you with clear reporting and analytics from a single interface. The fact that sales management software will help you manage all of your sales across multiple marketplaces without the need to log in and out of multiple sites can potentially save you hours per day. Professional marketplace sellers rarely log in to their Amazon or eBay seller accounts.

Sales management software will also help you manage your sales across your own eCommerce site which we will discuss later in this book.

IMPORTANT: Sales management software will require a solid investment in time and resource to set up and get running. It will also add to the cost of your online operation in terms of set-up fees, subscription fees and (in some cases) a fee based on a percentage of sales generated through the system. Before signing any contract with a software provider, you should make sure you have the resource to commit to this considerable investment and available margin to cover the costs.

GOING GLOBAL

Once you have mastered the domestic market on both eBay and Amazon, you might want to consider opening up your services to international customers. Doing this could be as simple as extending your delivery options to include international destinations. More sophisticated sellers will however wish to list their products directly on the international marketplaces of eBay and Amazon.

Selling internationally opens up a whole new can of worms regarding listing translation, customer services, tax liability, VAT, customs clearance, local payment options, warehousing, etc. Again, taking a slow and steady approach to international markets is recommended. Specialist companies such as InterCultural Elements (http://www.intercultural-elements.eu/) can advise you on suitable markets and cultural nuances as well as help you to implement your global expansion plans.

ONLINE RESOURCES FOR MARKETPLACE SELLERS

One of the great things about selling via online marketplaces is the vast community of sellers (who come from all walks of life), many of who are only too happy to share their stories and advice for finding success across the popular sales platforms. A handful of these sellers have gone one step further and built successful online publishing businesses providing detailed and incredibly valuable information for online sellers (regardless of their experience).

Here are just a few of the best independent, online resources and communities that I wholeheartedly endorse:

TameBay – http://www.tamebay.com
TameBay is a news and information service focusing mainly on eBay, Amazon and associated industries, but also includes news on the wider realm of eCommerce and online marketing. Managed by self-confessed eBay obsessives Chris Dawson and Dan Wilson (Dan was part of the team that founded eBay UK in 1999 and is also the author of the excellent book: *Make Serious Money on eBay UK, Amazon and Beyond* (ISBN: 978-1857886085)), who I would argue probably know more about selling via the online marketplaces than any single person employed by the online marketplaces themselves.

Highly Recommended: TameBay also publishes a free annual directory called The TameBay Guide. The guide features an incredibly wide range of tools and services for eBay, Amazon and eCommerce sellers. The directory is free and available via: http://tamebayguide.com/.

Understandinge – http://www.understandinge.com
Understandinge is an online educational resource for marketplace sellers who want to take their businesses to the next level. Operated by Matthew Ogborne and Dave Furness, two of the hardest working and most passionate eCommerce entrepreneurs I know (and both nice guys to boot).

Web Retailer – http://www.webretailer.com
A fantastic resource, compiled by Andy Geldman, featuring a detailed directory of peer reviewed services available to online marketplace and eCommerce sellers. Whether you are looking for a design service, help with selecting your multi-channel retail software supplier, a new courier or even finance solutions for your online marketplace business, you are sure to find it here.

eSeller – http://www.eseller.net
Primarily targeting businesses taking their first steps into the world of eCommerce, eSeller is brought to you by the publishers of the more enterprise business focused Internet Retailing magazine (http://www.internetretailing.net). Check out their free eBooks and occasional webinars for detailed "How to" guides to eCommerce.

eCommerceBytes – http://www.ecommercebytes.com
Originally known as AuctionBytes, eCommerceBytes is a US-based news and information service focusing on eBay, Amazon and associated services. Don't let the end of the last century look and feel to the site put you off, behind the bad design is a site packed with great advice and the home of a thriving community of online sellers.

Enterprise Nation – http://www.enterprisenation.com
Although not specifically targeted at online marketplace sellers, Enterprise Nation features detailed content that speaks directly to both micro and small business owners and covers many marketplace-relevant issues such as tax, cross-border sales, available grants, etc. (we should never forget an online business is a very real business). Enterprise Nation is also very big on community. When you sell online it is all too easy to find yourself so absorbed in the online world that you lose contact with the real world. Being part of an active community is vitally important (for your sanity, if nothing else).

ALTERNATIVE MARKETPLACES
While most small businesses will find a space on the mighty Amazon or eBay to sell their wares, there are a small number

of alternative marketplaces that are worth taking a look at to spread your online reach.

Etsy – http://www.etsy.com
Etsy is an online marketplace specialising in handmade and vintage items. It is also a great resource for crafting tools and supplies. Etsy has a huge community of followers who are looking for something unique, quirky, fun or just plain different from the mainstream.

Rakuten – http://www.rakuten.co.uk
An online marketplace that falls neatly between the eBay and Amazon experience. Rakuten allows its traders to open unique branded online stores within its portal, giving retailers a greater degree of freedom in terms of how their products are merchandised. Rakuten is particularly strong in the entertainment sector (books, CDs, and DVDs).

AbeBooks – http://www.abebooks.co.uk
Formerly known as the Advanced Book Exchange, AbeBooks is an online marketplace for booksellers listing used, rare, out-of-print and, increasingly, a growing number of new books.

NotOnTheHighStreet – http://www.notonthehighstreet.com
As the name suggests, this online marketplace does not cater to high street multiples or retailers selling mass-produced items. There is however a considerable opportunity for artisan or craft-type businesses to reach a sizeable audience (attracted by high volume online, outdoor and TV advertising). NotOnTheHighStreet boasts that their most successful customers have grown up to businesses turning over more than £1 million annually. For those of you who love a good inspirational, entrepreneurial story, it's refreshing to learn

that NotOnTheHighStreet has grown from a "kitchen table" business set up by two friends to one that now employs more than 120 staff (http://www.notonthehighstreet.com/about).

Warning: Despite often being an entry point for many retailers entering the world of eCommerce, selling via online marketplaces can be incredibly arduous. Beyond all the listing and re-listing or products (which can be automated), online marketplace customers can ask a lot of stupid questions, demand frequent updates on a product's delivery status and have great potential for leaving negative feedback, potentially damaging your reputation and impacting your product's visibility (that's two strikes against you). Selling via online marketplaces can prove to be quite an education, but should stand you in good stead once ready to spread your wings into the wider world of eCommerce (which in many ways can be much easier).

> *Selling via online marketplaces can prove to be quite an education, but should stand you in good stead once ready to spread your wings into the wider world of eCommerce*

CHAPTER 4 - BUILDING YOUR OWN ONLINE EMPIRE

As your multi-channel online business grows, many retailers (often stung by the high costs of selling via the online marketplaces) will be tempted to build their own online stores. They assume if they can factor out any listing, final value fees or sales commissions charged by the online marketplaces and sell direct to their customers via their own website, they will see greater profits.

In theory they are right, but in practice this is much more difficult (and expensive) than it might first appear.

Building a website can actually be very easy. Services like Magento (http://www.magento.com), Big Commerce (http://www.bigcommerce.com) or Volusion (http://www.volusion.com) provide very easy to use eCommerce systems which you can run independently or integrate with your multi-channel software management system (ask your vendor which platforms they integrate with) powering your eBay and Amazon sales without breaking the bank and with limited technical or design skills.

WEBSITE DESIGN: KEEP IT SIMPLE AND DON'T TRY TO RE-INVENT THE WHEEL

While it is possible to set up a basic online store with the basic (often free) templates that come packaged with many eCommerce packages, companies hoping to present a more credible image will want to create a customised online store front to represent their brand and attract more discerning customers.

Too many small retailers believe they need to do something different to stand out online. They think that they need to push the boundaries of design and technology when building their first eCommerce website. Many employ the services of inexperienced web designers who do not have the confidence to tell their clients to scale back their plans. Others are sold bespoke technology to manage their Web stores which they do not need, is expensive and makes it difficult for them to change their technology suppliers if they become unsatisfied with the service or their eCommerce vendor simply disappears (and this happens more often than you would believe).

If you have the desire to completely turn the world of eCommerce on its head, I urge you to take a look at your favourite websites and see how even the biggest brands like to keep things simple. In an age increasingly dominated by mobile technology, getting your website to display well on mobile phones and tablet computers should be your number one priority. Mobile friendly design is often referred to as "responsive design".

When engaging the services of a designer to customise the appearance (or skin) of your eCommerce store, you should be wary of anyone preaching anything beyond the mantra "Less is more". The very best designers will come equipped with multiple references (as will anyone else who claims they can help you with your online efforts).

THE YOUNG ONES (THE WRONG 'UNS)

If I had a dollar for every time an otherwise completely sane business person told me that they were entrusting their website operation to a niece or nephew (or a friend's son or daughter) who is "a whizz with computers", I would be a lot closer to retiring than I am now.

While most "young people" do "get" computers – this does not always mean they are best fit to build and manage what has the potential to drive significant revenues. Good web designers or software engineers are highly skilled individuals and come at a much higher premium than your "young" friends and family.

BUILD IT AND THEY MIGHT NOT COME

Online retail is not a field of dreams (referencing the classic baseball move). In the online world, it's not a case of build it and they will come because, more often than not, they will not. Like I said in the first chapter of this book, running an online business is not as easy as many people would have you believe and generating quality traffic (that converts to sales) is just about one of the most difficult things facing any retailer.

There is a very good reason why eBay and Amazon charge so much for retailers to sell their goods via their platforms. They have an incredible number of shoppers visiting their pages every day and they are trusted by consumers thanks to a reputation built up over many years of online trading. When you build your own website, unless you are a major brand, you are just another website littering the Web that nobody has heard of. Yes, you can pay for traffic via paid search or optimise your pages via an extensive Search Engine Optimisation (SEO) programme – but this is (a) very expensive and (b) doesn't build trust. In this respect, the Internet is more like the high street than you might initially believe, with some real estate being worth more than others.

GENERATING TRAFFIC

This might be an area where the traditional retailer has an advantage (albeit limited) over their online competitors (particularly when in start-up mode). While the online retailer has to start from scratch, an established high street retailer has a foundation (at least in the locations they operate) in terms of reputation and real estate where they can promote their online operation. Thinking back to the concept of curb appeal, if you are unable to make that car stop, at least you can make it known that you also sell online.

High street retailers will want to maximise on their traffic generating ability by ensuring their website address or uniform resource locator (URL) is clearly displayed in their window displays throughout the shop, on their point-of-sale signage and carrier bags (taking their online brand to the street).

TAKING THE LOCATION OUT OF YOUR URL

Your URL should be both short and memorable. In the perfect world, repeat visitors will arrive at your website directly via your URL as opposed to relying on search engines like Google, which will add to your costs and where you will be potentially ranked (favourably or otherwise) alongside your competitors. While a local business might focus on their geographic location (or the name of a proprietor) in their business name, a website has no geographic restrictions and visitors from outside of your traditional area of business are unlikely to identify with your family name (regardless of how well known you are locally). Therefore, there is little value (with a few exceptions) in using such naming conventions in your website address.

A great URL will tell your potential shoppers exactly what they are getting when they visit your site and may help your site become more visible on the major search engines.

Note: While many large online brands drive consumers to their websites using seemingly completely irrelevant (and sometimes quite bizarre) URLs, they often have huge marketing budgets to generate awareness and drive sales. If you are operating on a limited budget, it's probably best to keep your URL nice and simple and relevant to your line of business.

PAID SEARCH

Paid search delivers the small (often text-based) adverts you see at the top and on the side of search engine results pages (SERPS). Paid search adverts are sold by an auction system with the best positioned adverts going to advertisers based on a number of systems including relevance, cost and click-through rate (CTR). This means a carefully crafted, well targeted advert that generates a lot of clicks may well be cheaper and appear in a more prominent position than a badly written and poorly targeted campaign.

The paid search networks make their money every time someone clicks on an advert. The cost of a click can be anything from a couple of pence to many tens of pounds depending on the competition for the keyword you are bidding on.

Make no mistake, paid search advertising is not cheap and because (a) people will click on multiple ads, multiple times and (b) there is no guarantee of a sale following a click, it can quickly destroy your profits and, if left unchecked, damage your business.

I have personally worked with a number of large high street retailers with significant online brands who **DO NOT** see a profit from their paid search activity. As a general rule of thumb, the more competition there is for a product or service, the smaller the margin will be and the higher the advertising cost. Companies selling financial services or household items such as consumer electronics or domestic appliances may find the paid search advertising market particularly punishing. Large brands with large paid search budgets are playing a much longer game (one that few smaller businesses can afford to get involved with).

In the small business world, I have worked with many people who have had their fingers burnt with paid search. One business owner, who shall remain nameless to spare his blushes, once told me that he would have been better off digging a hole in his garden and throwing in several thousands of pounds of cash than investing in paid search. Another entrepreneur compared paid search to crack cocaine, in that it is expensive, provides a big hit and always left the user wanting more.

This is not to say that paid search is a waste of time or money. Paid search is a valuable acquisition marketing tool, but must be followed up with more cost effective, retention marketing techniques such as email marketing which will help deliver profits two or three sales down the line. Remember, it will always be more expensive to acquire new customers than to retain existing ones. Many small businesses will struggle to invest in long-term strategies like this. In such cases, paid search campaigns are best kept limited or not to be used at all.

EMAIL MARKETING

Email marketing remains the most cost effective method of driving repeat traffic to your website. Despite its maturity (it's been around for about 36 years and is older than the Internet as most of us would recognise) and the negative impact of spam email, email gives more recent online marketing techniques such as paid search, social media marketing and SEO a run for their money. We will talk more about email marketing in chapter seven of this book. For more insight into building strategic email marketing campaigns for your business check out my book: *A Crash Course in Email Marketing for Small and Medium-sized Businesses* (ISBN: 978-1908003713).

SOCIAL MEDIA MARKETING

Despite being relatively new on the scene, social media sites like Facebook and Twitter have become completely ingrained into our everyday lives. While much of the touted rise of fCommerce (eCommerce on Facebook) has fallen short on their promises, there can be no doubt in the traffic generating and reputation building ability of the major social media sites.

As the name suggests, social media is a venue where users go to socialise with friends and family. In this social environment your "friends", "followers" or "fans" may not appreciate being actively sold to. The most successful businesses on social media use the platform to share ideas, start conversations, solve problems and manage customer service issues. Selling is a by-product of this engagement.

Social media works at its very best when it is executed alongside a strategic campaign of email and content marketing (see below).

CONTENT MARKETING

As the name suggests, content marketing drives people to your website through the creation of compelling content. Content may be delivered in a number of formats including blog posts, online video (YouTube), images, product reviews, etc. Your content marketing strategy may also include developing relationships with journalists, bloggers and social media influencers (and customers) who can help promote your business. To learn more about this very modern approach to PR (which I often refer to as Thought Leadership Marketing) you might want to check out my first book: Becoming THE Expert: Enhancing Your Business Reputation through Thought Leadership Marketing (ISBN: 978-1908003614).

SEO

SEO is an art/science/scheme employed by many website operators to maximise their returns from natural search (the free listings on the major search engine results pages). While there is no cost associated with any traffic generated from natural search, SEO is not free. The time you invest in building an SEO strategy will be considerable and due to the fact that the likes of Google constantly move the goal posts to guarantee the quality of their search results, it's an ongoing effort.

WARNING: While there are many reputable SEO agencies out there, the industry is tarnished with a large number of unscrupulous "SEO experts" who operate "boiler room" style sales operations and offer little or no value to justify their monthly fees (neatly secured behind lengthy, watertight contracts). Always seek references before hiring the services of an SEO agency and be wary of those who seek to "game" the system with "Black Hat" SEO techniques. While these might have short-term success, they can ultimately lead to your company's complete removal from search engine results pages (nobody wants this).

As SEO evolves, it is becoming more reliant on marketers producing great content and as such SEO and content marketing can often be considered in the same breath.

AFFILIATE MARKETING

Affiliate marketing is a performance based marketing system where a vendor (retailer) rewards online publishers (including a diverse range of blogs, comparison shopping sites and online communities) for driving sales and other online activities (such as visits, lead generation, etc.) by paying out a referral fee or small commission on any sales made. Affiliate marketing has been around for a long time, but became big news online when Amazon rolled out their associates program in 1996. While affiliate marketing is a Cost Per Acquisition (CPA) marketing strategy (meaning that vendors only pay out on successful sales or the completion of clearly defined engagements), setting up an affiliate program via an Affiliate Marketing Network partner (who will manage the promotion of your program and provide the technology to track engagements and reward publishers) can be expensive.

Note: For an idea of just how big affiliate marketing is, consider the fact that hugely successful online brands like MoneySavingExpert.com, TripAdvisor.co.uk and CompareTheMarket.com are built on the back of affiliate marketing schemes.

The website PerformanceIN – (http://www.performancein.com) provides a valuable resource for retailers and publishers hoping to maximise their exposure and sell more via affiliate marketing.

Remember: There is no such thing as cheap or expensive marketing. There is only marketing that works and marketing that doesn't work. All online marketing technologies can be tracked, analysed, tested and then optimised or culled accordingly. The days of paying for advertising/marketing that does not deliver the kind of results you desire are over. Be very wary of salespeople trying to tie you into long-term contracts, if you have no or little experience of the technology.

CHAPTER 5 – WHEN BRICKS AND MORTAR HOLD YOU BACK

Many high street and online retailers believe their businesses are limited by the physical size of their stores/warehouses. They surmise that the bigger their facilities, the more items they can hold in stock and the more they can sell. While this might be true, I prefer to look at it another way. Holding too much stock in your own warehouse is expensive and will make your operation sluggish and inefficient.

IS YOUR WAREHOUSE/STOCKROOM AN ASSET OR A BURDEN?

As the majority of retailers make most of their money during relatively short peak sales periods, investing heavily in warehousing, retail space and staffing levels to meet this demand can be crippling. I see this happen a lot.

Retailers invest significant funds to enable them to maximise their results over a peak selling period (such as Christmas). They increase the size of their warehouses, they hire more staff, they ramp up their marketing budgets and they get really busy turning over significant sums of money. But this joy is short-lived as peak periods end and retailers are left with half-empty warehouses and idle staff (who inevitably will have to be let go), costing your business money and destroying the morale of those who survive the cull.

Sadly, both on the high street and in online retail, there are many busy fools. I believe there are four common traits of the busy fool, these are:

1. **Works Hard, Doesn't Understand Costs:** Puts everything into building their business but doesn't keep their eye on costs. Margins on individual products might be great, but when you factor in things like rent, insurance, wages, packaging, cleaning and even everyday essentials like tea, coffee and toilet paper, your business might not be so strong. Too many busy fools concentrate on turnover while failing to monitor actual profits.

2. **Doesn't Delegate/Outsource:** There are certain jobs that do not add value to your business. I believe you should concentrate on what you are passionate about and outsource everything else. For example, doing your own accounts may cost you more money than giving the work to a skilled accountant.

3. **Enjoys Manual Labour:** Technology can make your life so much simpler by automating many of the laborious tasks involved with running a retail business and freeing your time up to do more important things, like keeping your customers happy or sourcing the best products at the best price.

4. **Ignores Existing Clients:** It is much easier to make money out of your existing client base than to win new customers. Ignoring your existing clients to purely focus on acquiring new ones is, at the very best, foolish.

YOU DON'T MAKE MONEY STUFFING ENVELOPES

Successful online retailers will tell you that they don't make money shipping goods. Shipping goods is a time consuming and expensive operation which can destroy profits. Before you factor in the human cost of stuffing envelopes and packages, unless you have the buying power of the likes of Amazon, packaging materials are expensive to buy and take up valuable storage space (again costing you money).

Many smart online retailers often take advantage of virtual warehouse solutions such as FBA (http://bit.ly/1fWQvug). These services allow online retailers to scale up and down according to demand. This means they don't have to pay for warehouse space they only need during peak times or worry about hiring and firing staff to cope with seasonal adjustments in business.

Other benefits of outsourcing your warehousing and fulfilment include:

- Access to preferential delivery rates only available to high volume sellers

- Professional customer service agents on tap to handle things when they go wrong

- The ability to seamlessly handle returns (online retailers must offer this service under distance selling regulations)

- Increased visibility on Amazon (when using FBA)

Useful Tip: FBA can be employed to deliver goods sold via any channel (not just Amazon) including eBay, your own website, via the telephone or even in your high street retail store.

I have personally worked with a handful of online retailers who outsource all their warehousing, fulfilment and customer service operations, allowing them to concentrate on the buying and marketing of their products. In one case, this allows a significant international retail business to be run from a home office in the UK and (for six months a year) a villa in Spain. Yes – some online retailers really are living the dream.

Online Retail #Fail: Not all online retailers get it right. I once spent the afternoon with a desperate online seller who was on the verge of losing his business. He had access to great products and had the skills and knowhow to sell them in sufficient enough quantities which should have rewarded him royally. His problem was simple. His business was situated in North London where warehouse space (and his was sizeable) comes at a premium. His costs were ruining any chances of remaining competitive and he was losing most of his business to more favourably located businesses where rents were much (MUCH) lower. My advice was simple: Move! In the online world this is actually quite an easy option. Warehouse location rarely impacts sales and just because he relocated his warehouse operation does not mean he would have to uproot his family. I have worked with several entrepreneurs who successfully manage their online retail empires remotely from different cities, countries and even continents to their warehouse location.

Online Retail Success Case Study: Chris runs a successful online retail business from his home office which, for six months of the year, is located in the north of England. During the cold winter months he relocates his business (essentially just a laptop) to Malaga in Spain. His warehouse operations (which are entirely outsourced) are located in Bristol in the UK, his suppliers are mainly in China and his customer service agents (all freelancers hired from online services like oDesk and Elance) are located around the globe using Internet-based telephone systems to ensure his global customer base is served around the clock. The main reason why he doesn't operate his own warehouse or employ full-time staff is so that he can exercise greater flexibility over his costs and can expand and retract his business as and when required without incurring costs. Chris sees himself first and foremost as a skilled buyer and marketer. He works the hours that suit him and rarely even sees the stock he sells. In short, Chris is living the dream. But be warned, this didn't come easy. It took many years to build up his business, put systems in place so that everything runs smoothly and learn to trust his outsourced help so he can effectively leave his business for significant periods of time to run itself. If you want this kind of lifestyle, you've got to be prepared to put in the work.

While not everyone will be comfortable taking Chris' hands-off approach to business, there are a number of strategies you can adopt to make your business life more efficient.

THE 4-HOUR WORK WEEK

I recently read Timothy Ferriss' excellent book, *The 4-Hour Work Week*. It's not a new title, and I've got to admit, I initially treated the book with a degree of scepticism, but I was encouraged to download a copy by a good friend whose opinion I trust and who, like me, has no desire to abandon the workplace.

Ferriss' approach to creating a decent work/life balance (he calls it "lifestyle design") might be a little extreme for some (and completely unrealistic to others), but it's a great read packed with a number of tips that I believe can help us all become more efficient marketers.

While Ferriss uses many of the strategies in his book to escape work (while retaining positive cash flow in his business) so he can concentrate on traveling the world, studying new languages and cultures, entering and winning martial arts competitions, and even learning to dance the tango, I believe many of his tips could just help us to get more out of the working day and create a little more fun time on the side.

If Ferriss can achieve so much in his professional life in as little as four hours per week, imagine what you can do in 40 hours with a little adjustment to your working routine.

10 PRODUCTIVITY HACKS TO MAKE YOUR BUSINESS MORE EFFICIENT

1. **Meetings:** Unless absolutely necessary, meetings should be avoided (especially if you are simply meeting out of habit). If they cannot be avoided, meetings should start and end on time (if not earlier) and not deviate from the pre-proposed agenda.

2. **Email Management:** You should manage your email and not be managed by it. Dedicate a small amount of

time each day to the process and whenever possible, instead of contributing to long chains of email conversations, try picking up the phone or directly speaking to someone.

3. **Email Autoresponders:** Set people's expectations of when they can expect to hear back from you (if at all) through careful use of email autoresponders. It might be possible to direct some email enquiries to an FAQ page on your website that will help them address any queries without the need to send a reply.

4. **The 80/20 Rule:** The Pareto Principle suggests that you should focus your efforts on the 20% of your business activities that generate 80% of your revenue. Try and eradicate the activities that consume the most time, but generate little in return.

5. **Escape the Office:** Try working from home from time to time. You might find escaping the workplace and all its distractions makes you more productive.

6. **Outsource:** Don't be a busy fool. Farm out any time-consuming or repetitive tasks to a freelance contractor. By freeing up your time, you'll be able to concentrate on more appropriate/lucrative tasks.

7. **Screen Your Calls:** Unless you work in a customer-facing role, don't answer any calls from telephone numbers you don't recognise. If it is important, they will call you back or send an email.

8. **Test:** Beta tests and soft launches allow you to see if a strategy works without investing too much time, effort or money on big projects that could potentially go nowhere.

9. **Invest in Technology:** Great technology will not only help you free up your time, it will help you become a more creative and passionate marketer by automating many of the processes and repetitive tasks that eat into your day and destroy your morale.

10. **Live for Your Passion:** Focus the majority of your efforts on a niche and become known for your expertise in this area.

While becoming more efficient should go some way to making you more successful and happy in your work, at the end of the day the truly successful amongst us find balance in everything they do. Consider the following:

A SIMPLE FORMULA FOR FINDING HAPPINESS IN WHATEVER YOU DO

I'm lucky, I enjoy my job and have a good home life, so if you ask me if I am happy, I'll gladly tell you, "Most of the time". While I enjoy a good work-life balance (largely by breaking the shackles of nine-to-five employment), I didn't have a secret formula that I could bottle and sell (if only you could).

It was a simple phone-in debate on the radio discussing the concept of happiness and whether government should be held responsible for ensuring its delivery that suggested to me the problem of guaranteeing happiness was much simpler.

A caller suggested that true happiness wasn't connected to wealth, success or social standing. Instead, to be truly happy you must have three things:

1. **Something to love** (This could be family, friends or even a pet).

2. **Something to do** (A job, a hobby, time spent volunteering or in education).

3. **Something to look forward to** (A holiday, a social event, a regular meeting with friends).

I wondered if this could be behind the reason why my postman greets me every morning with a tuneful whistle and the young man who works such long hours at my local convenience store always wears a smile on his face. Perhaps they discovered this "secret" formula before I did.

PUTTING CUSTOMERS' HAPPINESS FIRST

In the retail environment, we should always put the customers' happiness before our own. Unfortunately for many bricks and mortar retailers, their online competition is winning the game here as well. So how do you compete with online retailers in the happiness stakes? In the next chapter we look at how traditional retail can level the playing field and get people smiling again.

CHAPTER 6 – CUSTOMER CARE

Thanks to initiatives like The Distance Selling Regulations in the UK, customers of online stores actually have more protection in the online environment than they do on the high street.

Distance selling regulations state that a consumer who buys a product online (with a handful of exceptions including financial products, fresh produce or personalised items) have the right to return that item and receive a full refund (up to 14 days after receipt) without giving any reason. This could mean the consumer has simply changed his or her mind and no longer wants the product.

This right of return is not always available on the high street. While many retailers will offer a "no questions asked" return policy, offering an exchange or a credit note (as opposed to cash), they are not legally obliged to.

Retail Fail: While standing in a customer service queue in a well-known UK DIY store to purchase a patio gas canister refill, I was disgusted with the way the sales assistant and store manager treated a customer returning a lawn mower. The item, which had been recommended by a sales assistant, had two settings allowing the user to select how long or short they wished to cut their lawn. The customer told the sales assistant that these settings either left his lawn too long or hacked up the ground under the grass. Essentially, the lawn mower was not fit for purpose. The sales assistant took the lawn mower from its packaging, plugged it in and turned it on. The blades turned and the sales assistant told the customer that there was nothing wrong with the product and she couldn't offer a refund or exchange. The customer then went on to explain for the next 15 minutes why the lawn mower was not fit for purpose before the manager was called (during which time the queue of customers behind the perplexed customer grew even longer). The manager, who spoke to the customer with complete contempt, agreed with the sales assistant and refused to back down. In desperation, the customer pulled up the company's website on his mobile phone and showed the manager a selection of negative reviews of the product (which he had read after purchasing and attempting to use the product). The manager then proceeded to laugh at the customer and ask why he had bought a product with such bad reviews. The customer walked out without receiving a refund, an exchange or even a civil word from the store's staff, vowing to take his complaints further up the chain. I, and most of the people standing in the queue behind me, left the store vowing never to shop there again. Had the customer bought the item online he could have simply returned it for a full refund, no questions asked and everyone else in the customer services queue (including myself) would have all had a less stressful Sunday afternoon. Wouldn't life be simpler if the high street operated in the same way?

TRY BEFORE YOU BUY

While the above is perhaps at the extreme end of poor

customer service, it is just one example of why I personally prefer to shop online (particularly for more expensive items). The days of bricks and mortar retailers having an advantage over their online competition because customers can touch and feel a product before they commit to purchase are over. Online retailers offering free delivery and equally important, free, no quibble return policies (backed by consumer law and the securities afforded by making purchases using a credit card) completely remove any risk.

SHOWROOMING - HOW REAL WORLD RETAILERS CAN FIGHT BACK

How many real world businesses pride themselves on offering unrivalled product knowledge and amazing customer service? Make no mistake, the general public really appreciate this service and will often spend many hours consulting with real world retailers prior to going online (often, adding insult to injury, while still standing in the retailer's premises) and making a purchase. This process is often referred to as showrooming and it should be a major concern for any real world retailer.

To prevent showroomers from taking free advantage of your expertise and then rewarding your online competition, consider the following options:

- **Challenge Online Prices:** Try to match the price of any reasonable offer available online. Remember to take into account the cost of delivery and any optional extras such as extended warranties. While it might hurt to reduce your margins, it is better to take a smaller profit than to give business away. Don't cut your nose off to spite your face but remember, stock sitting on your shelves is costing you money and potentially losing value every day it remains unsold.

- **Offer Free Delivery:** Get back to basics and offer free delivery at a time to suit your customers' needs. If a product needs installing, offer to do that for free as well. We'll look at adding value to your service with delivery options later in this chapter.

- **What's the Point (of Sale):** Make sure your customers know you are in the game by ensuring all your point-of-sale signage features a clear call to action (CTA). A good CTA might say: "Ask us about our free delivery service", "Ask us to match any price online" or "Cannot find what you are looking for? Ask us and we'll order it today for free home delivery".

- **Take the Fight Online:** If all else fails, make sure your stock is also available online and can be found online by showroomers. Offer free Wi-Fi to your customers to make the process even easier and show just how competitive your business is. If your point-of-sale and added-value services are doing the job – you'll have little to worry about.

THE PRICE IS RIGHT

Because competition is so fierce online, pricing can best be described as fluid, with retailers constantly cutting costs to remain competitive. Some might see this approach as a race to the bottom and if you sell products that are universally available (things like CDs or books, computer games or consumer electronics), it can be very hard to compete (or make a profit) with this constant discounting.

It can also be very labour-intensive to monitor and update pricing, and have any chance of competing. Again this is an area where technology can help you.

Repricing software can help online retailers remain viable on highly competitive market places like Amazon by automatically scanning the competition and adjusting pricing accordingly (following strict business rules, so you don't completely destroy your margins – unless you just want to clear stock). For a full list of repricing software solutions check out this post on WebRetailer: http://bit.ly/1hMlnAV

Despite a culture of deep discounts, sometimes being the cheapest seller doesn't always make sense. While the heaviest discounter might shift their stock incredibly quickly, when they inevitably run out of stock (or go bankrupt as many are prone to do), your more reasonably priced goods (with better margins) will fill the void. Online marketplaces like Amazon don't always position products based on price and reward increased visibility to retailers based on a number of other factors such as available quantity, delivery options (FBA is a clear advantage here) and customer feedback/reputation.

Remember: A fluid pricing strategy can mean (depending on product demand) the price of stock can go up as well as down.

Repricing software will help you find balance between the right price and your optimum sales numbers.

BIG BOX RETAILERS AND THEIR ONLINE ALIASES

Many big box retailers don't like the concept of competing with their online rivals on price because they want to protect their margins in their expensive high street stores. In an age where everyone carries an Internet-enabled smart phone in their pocket and can try in-store before they buy online (or showroom), they are fighting a losing battle.

While many larger successful retailers are embracing a multi-channel retail strategy, creating seamless brands across the high street and online properties, others chose a more risky approach and (this might sound crazy) are actually competing against themselves online by attempting to maintain their rigid high street pricing strategy at the same time as offering discounted products via a range of online aliases.

One company who engaged in this rather bizarre business practice was the failed UK electrical retailer Comet who fell into administration in 2012.

As a rule, Comet did not actively compete with their online competition. While Comet did have a solid eCommerce operation, the prices available online matched the prices available on the high street, resulting in them appearing very uncompetitive.

However, realising they had to compete against up and coming online rivals, they decided to launch a number of discount online operations using aliases such as Kitchen Science and Laskys. To my mind, this strategy made little sense. Consumers will often visit many websites before making a buying decision. As we have already eluded in this book, the cost of attracting visitors is expensive. Paying to attract customers to three or four different sites and then competing against yourself on price is simply ridiculous and history reveals how this sorry story unfolded.

The moral of this story is that if you are unwilling or unable to compete on price, you'd better find something else to compete on. Remember, customers don't always buy on price. If you can offer exceptional service or add something additional in terms of customer experience, focus on what makes you different and worth the extra expense. This theory is perhaps best supported by the fact that many luxury goods retailers actually thrived during the downturn while many of their more reasonably priced cohorts floundered.

THE IMPACT OF SOCIAL MEDIA ON CUSTOMER CARE AND YOUR REPUTATION

Businesses that fail to update their customer service strategies risk the wrath of a social media backlash. Poor customer service will not only lose you the customers who are impacted by your failings, thanks to social media your wider reputation is at risk. Maintaining a solid reputation is vitally important in this socially-enabled age. In this respect, carefully managing your social media activity is very much part of a wider reputation management or PR strategy.

We'll talk more about social media in chapter eight of this book.

ADDED VALUE DELIVERY OPTIONS BOLSTER ONLINE REPUTATION

It might surprise you to learn that online retailers have very little control over an area of business which has the most potential to damage their reputation. Once a product has left an online retailers warehouse, their reputation is very much in the hands of the postal service or courier responsible for delivering the item.

We've all heard or maybe even experienced horror stories at the hands of couriers. Parcels left out in the rain, fragile items tossed over garden fences and the dreaded "sorry you were out" card posted through your letterbox when you've been waiting in for a delivery all day. Perhaps the most bizarre delivery story I have heard was from a friend who discovered a note from his courier saying his parcel had been left in his dustbin. Sadly, he discovered the note minutes after the local council refuse team had made their weekly collection.

When a courier loses, damages or delays the delivery of a parcel, it's the online retailer who suffers (both financially and in terms of reputation).

Understanding the risk involved with the delivery process, many online retailers are diligently working to not only improve the process, but also to add value to their online sales operations by offering a range of delivery options.

WHY FAST AND FREE IS NOT ALWAYS THE BEST OPTION

Free next day delivery is not always the best option particularly if a customer has to take time off work to wait for a package to arrive. Sometimes a customer will pay a premium to have an item delivered on a specific day and at a specific time.

Software companies like MetaPack - (http://www.metapack.com) – enable retailers to create multiple delivery options to suit their customers' specific needs. MetaPack also helps retailers select the best courier service based on criteria such as product weight and size, requested delivery time and cost of delivery. Technology like this not only helps online retailers optimise the delivery process, helping them to control shipping costs and offer a more flexible service to their customers by ensuring packages and parcels arrive on time, it takes some of the risk out of the delivery process and helps protect retailers' reputations.

CLICK AND COLLECT

Click and collect is big news for many clicks and mortar retailers (stores that have a strong presence online and on the high street). Essentially, it allows a customer to select and buy an item online before calling into a physical store. Click and collect gives retailers two bites at the cherry to make a sale. When a customer buys a product using click and collect from a website like Tesco Direct, they are very likely to make additional (perhaps impulse) purchases when they call into the store to pick up their orders.

But click and collect doesn't just represent a big opportunity for major brands with an extensive network of shops.

Services like Collect+ - (http://www.collectplus.co.uk) - allow online retailers of all shapes and sizes to take the risk out of home delivery by enabling online shoppers to collect (and if required return) their purchases from a vast network of high street convenience shops. Despite being an online brand, it could be argued that Collect+ offers much needed support to many traditional high street businesses, bringing much needed footfall and supplementary income to shops that might otherwise lose out to the supermarkets or online retailers.

THE FUTURE OF HOME DELIVERY

Thanks largely to the rapid growth of online retail, the parcel delivery industry is evolving at pace. Guaranteed delivery within a short window of time and same day delivery are becoming common place in many metropolitan areas. Even the news that online retail giant Amazon is trialling drones as a method of delivery might not seem too out there when you learn that DHL is already successful using drone aircraft to deliver packages to offshore locations in the North Sea (see: http://bit.ly/1qz1kDm).

CHAPTER 7 – CUSTOMER RETENTION – COME BACK SOON

As anyone who has been in business for any length of time will tell you, it is much easier (and more cost effective) to make money from an existing client than to win a new one. This means in both the real world and the online environment we must not only fight for every new piece of business that comes our way, we must also do our very best to ensure that once won, customers come back and continue to spend money.

It probably won't surprise you to learn that in this digital age, where customers can compare prices and availability of any products in just a couple of clicks, customer loyalty is at best, rather fickle.

While many real world businesses will pride themselves on their exceptional customer service and unrivalled product knowledge, your customers' long-term memory might not be so good. Particularly if they are being courted with lower costs and perhaps a more convenient shopping experience online.

One area where online retailers are way ahead of their real world counterparts is in their use of retention marketing (often powered by email marketing).

When a customer buys a product or service online, along with their name, address and payment details, they also provide their email address. This allows the online retailer to send them a receipt and advise on the delivery process. It also allows them to maintain contact with that customer with email marketing offers, helping to drive repeat purchases and generate something called Customer Lifetime Value (CLV).

High acquisition costs and wafer-thin margins might mean an online retailer does not see a profit from the first couple of sales to an individual client. This is especially true when new customers are won through expensive acquisition marketing techniques like paid search. Make no mistake, CLV is very important online and it should also be very important in your real world business.

EMAIL MARKETING

As a real world business you might think that an online technology like email marketing can only be used successfully by online brands. You'd be wrong. I have a long history in email marketing and one of the reasons I was initially attracted to the industry was the fact that I don't believe there is a single business that could not benefit from email marketing.

I have personally overseen successful email marketing campaigns for products as diverse as high-spec computer software and frozen chicken nuggets and everything in-between.

Email marketing remains the most cost effective marketing tool available to entrepreneurs. Email marketing might not be as new and sexy as social media, but it certainly packs a much bigger punch. According to the Direct Marketing Association's

Statistical Fact Book in 2013, email marketing campaigns delivered a staggering 4,300% return on investment (or $42.08 for every dollar spent). Compare this to any other form of marketing available to your business and try not to get too depressed that you didn't start email marketing earlier.

These fantastic results are of course based on marketers following best practices, many of which I talk about in my book: *A Crash Course in Email Marketing for Small and Medium-sized Businesses* (ISBN: 978-1908003713). Another useful resource which I contribute to is The iContact Blog – (http://www.icontact.com/blog) which is updated daily with email marketing best practices, industry trends and news, mostly relevant to the small business marketer.

SOME BASIC RULES REGARDING EMAIL

You cannot write about email without addressing the issue of spam.

Despite its prevalence, spam marketing simply doesn't work. This is because it lacks the basic principle of permission between the sender and recipient required to build and maintain a relationship.

Email marketing's success is based on the permission a customer has given you to contact them with relevant marketing offers. Permission is granted when a customer supplies their email details in the process of a sale or simply asks to be added to your mailing list. Online retailers collect email data as a matter of course. There is no reason why a real world retailer shouldn't do the same and find similar success with email marketing.

But before you start firing emails out to all and sundry, there are some very important rules you must follow:

IMPORTANT: You cannot build a list without permission. Sending email marketing messages without the express permission of the recipient is spam and spam is illegal. You have been warned.

IMPORTANT: Because permission is so important to the success of any email marketing campaign, you should never be tempted to buy a list of names. Even if the list broker has been given permission to sell these details because they have no previous relationship with your organisation, any email sent to a bought list is as good as spam.

IMPORTANT: Every email marketing message you send should include instructions for your subscriber to leave your list. Email marketing software like iContact – (http://www.icontact.com) - automatically adds unsubscribe links to every email they send and manage the process for you automatically. Everyday email tools like Outlook Express do not have this functionality and so should not be used for email marketing purposes. If you continue to send emails after a subscriber has opted-out, you are essentially sending spam.

IMPORTANT: When a subscriber joins your email list, they do so with the understanding that you will only send relevant, timely and engaging communications. The moment you start delivering content that goes off-piste you risk losing subscribers and may even be entering the world of, there's that word again, spam. This is especially important if you run a number of businesses. If for example you own a shop and a hotel, and your relationship with your subscriber is via the shop, you should only send email marketing messages regarding the shop.

As you might guess, those of us who work in the email marketing industry do not like spam. Spam damages the industry's reputation and ultimately could impact the future success of your business. Don't be a spammer.

A TALE OF TWO BICYCLE SHOPS

As anyone who reads my blogs or follows me on social media will know, I am a keen cyclist. In my home town there are two independently owned bike shops I could potentially visit to service my bike and make the occasional purchase.

Both shops offer a quick, efficient and highly professional service. They are fairly well-matched in terms of available products and stock, and are a similar distance from my house. There is very little difference between both shops, so why would I choose to visit one much more regularly than the other?

The simple answer is email marketing.

While bicycle shop #1 takes my money and lets me leave the shop, adopting the strategy of hope as their only effort to make me return, bicycle shop #2 makes a considerable effort to stay on my radar and win future business.

When I first visited shop #2 to buy a new winter cycling jacket (I was initially attracted to a highly visible promotion in the shop's window) they not only took the time to understand exactly what I was looking for (they even offered me a cup of coffee), they also invited me to open a free account which would have immediate benefits. In exchange for my email address, they would hold a record of all my previous purchases (useful if I ever had any problems and needed to make a return), email me my receipts and offer a 10% discount on all purchases including the one I was making that day. I would also receive an informative and interesting monthly email newsletter highlighting a range of products to suit the season, relevant local events and other great offers. I'd be a fool to decline such an offer.

Because their emails are so useful, I open them even when I'm not interested in buying something and (very occasionally) they will change my mind and I will make a purchase. The great thing about this one particular shop is they get the whole multi-channel retail thing, meaning I can go directly from their email newsletter to their website and buy a product and have the item shipped directly to my home or office or pop into the shop and pick it up.

I believe all great marketing (like all good products or services) should be useful. My favourite bike shop understands this and always attempts to be useful as opposed to simply selling. They use content as the bait and a good call-to-action as the hook to reel me in – and I'm happy to be caught in this manner.

Many real world businesses are afraid to ask for email details because they believe their customers will have a negative impression of email marketing. Keep it useful, like bicycle shop #2, and you'll have nothing to worry about.

UPDATE: Bicycle shop #1 has upped its game and started making an attempt to market itself to the local cycling community in my home town. They have taken to taping flyers to bikes chained up at bike racks throughout the town. There are a couple of reasons why I don't like this. Firstly it creates litter and secondly, I don't like people touching my bike when I leave it outside a shop. But this approach is also indiscriminate. The people taping flyers to bike handles have no idea if the bike belongs to an existing customer or not. The flyers do not build relationships and ultimately seem a little desperate. Wouldn't it be easier to ask for an email address and build reputation via word of mouth (more commonly distributed these days via social media)?

If you're still looking for an excuse not to engage your customers via email marketing, I doubt there is anything you could tell me that I have not heard before.

The following abridged blog post first appeared on Business2Comminuty (http://bit.ly/1uDCRnd):

7 Stupid Things People Say about Email Marketing

1. **We need to get into email marketing, it's the future:** Email marketing isn't the future; it's the here and now. It is, more than any other form of marketing, your best chance to drive revenues (and profits) from your existing clients and prospects.

2. **Email marketing is dead. It's all about social media now**: Rather than killing email, social media has strengthened its proposition. Social media is an amazing place to engage your clients and prospects in conversation, but it is not a great sales venue. This is because people don't like to be sold to in a social environment. Email, on the other hand, is very much a place of work where people not only expect to be sold to, they actively welcome it.

3. **Email marketing is dead. It's all about mobile now:** About 65% of all emails are opened on mobile devices. Like social media, mobile has also strengthened email marketing's proposition. Mobile has freed the inbox from the desktop, giving you a greater opportunity to hit your subscribers at a time and place when they are more likely to make a buying decision.

4. **I'm waiting until my list reaches critical mass before I send my first campaign:** The average age of an email address is 18 months. That means if you sit on a list for any length of time, your list will have decayed and will not be as big as you think it is. People also have short

memories. Just because someone had a relationship with you last year doesn't mean he or she will remember you when you finally make contact. Your most successful email will always be the first one you send following a registration or purchase. So remember to hit your subscribers while they are hot.

5. ***I'd like to give email marketing a try. Where can I buy a list?:*** You cannot buy a list. Email's success is based on the permission your list recipients have given you to contact them. When you buy a list, no matter what your broker tells you, you do not have permission to send commercial emails to its members, and your campaign will have all the hallmarks of a spam campaign.

6. ***I'm focusing all my efforts on paid search:*** Paid search is a fantastic acquisition channel but can be very expensive. The high cost of an individual click can very often destroy any profit margin you might have in a product or service. This is where email marketing comes in by driving repeat orders and increasing customer lifetime value. I like to think of email marketing as the profitable component of more expensive acquisition techniques. Remember, if you pay to acquire the same customers again and again, you may never see a profit from them.

7. ***I do email marketing. We send out a monthly newsletter:*** While the monthly newsletter does have a place in your email marketing strategy, it is not the be-all and end-all. In many cases it is an afterthought and as such is rushed and therefore lacks quality and is unlikely

to drive much in the way of engagement. Remember, email will only deliver a positive ROI when your campaigns are relevant, engaging and timely. This might mean putting a little more thought into your campaigns than you currently do with your newsletter.

 *Remember, email will only deliver a positive ROI when your campaigns are relevant, engaging and timely."*

CHAPTER 8 – LET'S GET SOCIAL

I've left social media towards the end of this book for a very good reason. This is because I believe that social media is neither the foundation nor structural makeup of any decent marketing strategy. Don't get me wrong, social media represents an amazing opportunity to engage your existing and potential customers in conversation, but there are many things I believe you should invest in first.

This is often brought home to me when I deliver my Content Marketing Boot Camp events (which have visited cities across the UK, Europe and US). I often start by asking my audience "Who is on social media?" Everyone raises their hands. I then ask, "Who blogs?" Only a handful of hands remain raised.

In my mind, this begs the question, if marketers are not investing in good content, what are they actually posting to social media?

Many of these (quite frankly lazy) marketers are simply using social to either bombard their followers with marketing offers and as we have already alluded to in chapter four, social media alone is not a great sales channel. Others, and this is just stupid, are actively driving people away from their brand by pointing people towards content produced by more savvy marketers.

SOCIAL MEDIA AND RETURN ON INVESTMENT

While social media provides many opportunities to engage your target audience, there is a common misconception that it is difficult (if not impossible) to deliver a positive return on investment from the medium.

The following abridged post first appeared on the ViralHeat Blog (http://bit.ly/1GOFtjX):

6 Places to Find Buried Treasure (ROI) on Social Media

If you are struggling to find ROI from your social media marketing efforts here are six places I suggest you look first:

1. **Customer Acquisition:** Social media provides an amazing opportunity to generate new business leads. These could come from an individual posing a question via a social media platform (such as: Can anyone recommend a good accountant in London?) or perhaps an existing client sharing a piece of content or general insight with their wider social network. Having the technology in place to monitor these conversations via the social web will make it easier to find these potentially profitable engagements and track revenues generated from them.

2. **Customer Retention:** As anyone who has been in business for any length of time will tell you, it's much easier to make money from an existing client than to win a new one. Social media will help you retain profitable relationships by helping you understand how your clients feel about your brand, your product

and your services and can help flag up problems before they become threats. Remember, a problem can become an opportunity if it is identified quickly and handled in the right way.

3. **Customer Services:** A vital component of any acquisition or retention strategy (see points #1 and #2). Social media is increasingly becoming a channel of choice for clients and potential *clients to contact your organisation. The public nature of social media communications mean that any contact via social media should be monitored and followed up accordingly. The best place to do this is through your existing contact centres where trained and experienced staff can efficiently handle inquiries and complaints, as well as monitoring and processing more general communications.*

4. **Public Relations:** *In recent years, social media has significantly disrupted the PR landscape. Journalists no longer have the monopoly over how news is disseminated. Organisations (and even individuals) with large social media followings can potentially yield the kind of influence only once afforded to major news networks. PR has traditionally been another area where it is difficult (but not impossible) to track ROI. If you see value in investing in any form of PR, social media should be seen as a vital component of that strategy.*

5. **Email Marketing:** *Social media was once seen as a major threat to the email marketing industry but is now more likely to be seen as a profitable bedfellow. Socialising*

your email content has the potential to increase the reach and effectiveness of your email marketing campaigns, essentially turning a traditional retention marketing channel into an extremely low cost acquisition marketing channel.

6. **Competitive Analysis:** *Sometimes the biggest opportunities happen when a competitor drops the ball and makes a mistake or comes up with an idea which you can exploit. Monitoring your competitors' social media activity will not only help you understand how the market feels about your industry in general, it could influence new revenue generating ideas.*

The moral of this story is that social media ROI is not part of some elaborate tale where the lines between reality and fantasy have been blurred by mystery and rumour. Social media should be an integral part of your organisation's revenue protection and growth strategies. The ROI is there, and the chances are you won't have to look too far to find it.

FINDING THE TIME TO GET SOCIAL

One of the biggest problems with social media is the fact it is like digital quicksand. One minute you might be updating your company Facebook page or Twitter feed, and the next thing you know you have been sucked in and lost yourself in a mire of conversations with friends, family and long-lost acquaintances. Commenting on images of a friend's cats or sharing images that encourage you to "like" this post if you love your daughter, mother, the 1970s, etc. etc. will not deliver a positive return on your time invested in being social.

I once spoke with a small business marketing consultant who told me that she knew she had the wrong people following her on social media because every time she posted something about work, there was little, if any, response but when she posted a photo of her cat, her feed went crazy. Because of this, I believe it is vitally important to separate your work life and your professional life on social media.

WHICH SOCIAL NETWORK IS RIGHT FOR YOUR BUSINESS?

While Facebook, Twitter, LinkedIn and Pinterest take most of the social media limelight, there are numerous other social media channels vying for your attention. It would be impossible to find the time to engage with them all and so it is best to select a couple of networks that suit your customers' (not necessarily your own) social needs and invest your time in building an audience via these channels.

Because I am in the business of engaging the business community, I find my own social media efforts are more lucrative when I engage people via Twitter and LinkedIn. I do have a Facebook page, but spend very little time updating it.

Retailers, or businesses working in a more visually stimulating sector (food, travel, entertainment, and fashion) might find Facebook more worthwhile and should certainly consider experimenting with Pinterest and Instagram.

To my shame, I do very little with Google+. This is almost certainly detrimental to my business because, I believe while Google+ has developed a bit of a reputation as a social media "also ran", anything you can do to get into bed with the search giant is highly likely to aid (it certainly won't do any harm) your rankings on their search results. While there are only so many hours in the day, Google+ (and YouTube – also owned by Google) is on my list of New Year's resolutions for 2015. Watch this space.

BUILDING AN AUDIENCE ON SOCIAL MEDIA

When building an audience on social media you should always remember, quality will always outweigh quantity. Better to have 100 fully engaged followers or fans than 1,000 virtual strangers who will only see your posts as an intrusion on their Facebook wall or Twitter feed. Therefore, buying fans and followers (the majority of which will be fake) or begging everyone in your inbox to "like" your Facebook page is little more than a misguided exercise in vanity.

Building any kind of community can be incredibly difficult and social media is no different. Many business owners believe that the simple act of being really active on social media will help them win new friends and perhaps help position them as influential thought leaders. And so, they post anything and everything that may or may not be loosely connected to their business. I often refer to these kind of social media marketers (and I use the term loosely) as wannabes. The wannabe constantly re-appropriates other people's content and ultimately drives potential customers away from their brand (occasionally into the hands of a competitor) out of sheer boredom.

I'll let you in on a little secret about building a following on social media. If you want to get more followers on social media, you really need to do something interesting off social media.

6 TIPS TO BUILD A FOLLOWING ON SOCIAL MEDIA

1. **Have a Great Product:** Everything starts with your product or service. If you don't have a great product or service (or equally important, believe in your own product or service) you most certainly will fail.

2. **Build Amazing Content:** Great content is the foundation of any successful social media marketing strategy. Invest in a good blog, take the time to write some decent posts, take your own photos, design eye-catching infographics to share and produce entertaining videos. Strive to do something creative every day and remember, content marketing is a marathon, not a sprint.

3. **Solve Customer Problems:** The best marketing solves problems for your clients and prospects. If you can solve a problem for a single client, there is a very good chance, once shared via social media, many others will benefit from your advice.

4. **Socialise in the Real World:** Get out there and meet real people. Build real relationships over a cup of

coffee or a glass of wine and your social media relationships will bloom.

5. **Speak:** Offer your services as an expert speaker at industry-related events and build your reputation in front of a live audience. An engaging speech will set your social media feed on fire.

6. **Support Bloggers and Journalists:** Having an independent blogger or journalist endorse your opinion will do absolutely no harm to your social media credibility.

The moral of the story is if you want to lead a successful life on social media, you may first need to live a little in the real world.

SOCIAL MEDIA'S ROLE IN YOUR RETENTION STRATEGY

The following abridged blog post first appeared on the iContact Email Marketing Blog - http://bit.ly/1yaBbPM .

Are You Asking Your Customers for Their Twitter Handles?

A friend asked me the other day if, in the past five years, I had ever been asked for my Twitter handle when buying a product. I laughed at the idea.

It wasn't the concept of asking your customers if they were on Twitter that I found so bizarre. In fact, it makes so much sense; I don't know why you wouldn't do it.

What I found so funny was that he was suggesting that businesses should ask for something so (relatively) modern when so many have been ignoring the opportunity represented by email for years.

Remember, email marketing—more than any other form of marketing—remains the most cost-effective method of driving repeat orders to your business.

I can honestly count on one hand the number of independent, brick-and-mortar retailers who have asked me for my email address while I made a purchase in the past decade.

Why these businesses seem so happy for me to walk away from their stores without identifying myself as a potential repeat customer is a mystery to me. It would never happen in the online environment.

Do online retailers value their customers more than traditional businesses?

Of course not, and let's be honest, many online businesses still haven't grasped the opportunity of regular and properly targeted email marketing campaigns.

If you are not asking your customers for their email addresses when they enter your stores, you are missing a huge opportunity. Worse still, if you are asking your customers for their email addresses and not doing anything with them, what are you thinking about?

Perhaps you (or your staff) might feel awkward about asking for an email address, but really what is the worst that can happen? I would personally feel more awkward about turning future sales away.

Try and incentivise your employees to collect email addresses with competitions and small bonuses. You should also incentivise your customers with the promise of great future deals and relevant content.

Get email right first and then—who knows?—you might make that bold step to engaging (note: the word is "engaging," not "broadcasting") with them via social media.

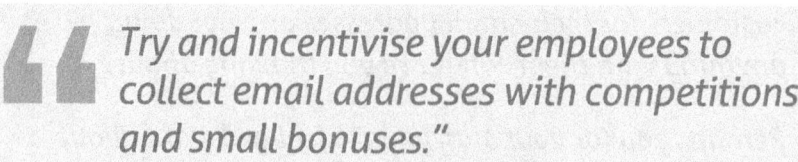

> Try and incentivise your employees to collect email addresses with competitions and small bonuses."

CHAPTER 9 – ALTERNATIVE STREAMS OF REVENUE

As we have discussed throughout this book, complacency is the greatest threat to your business.

Remember: No business has the God-given right to stay in business and so it is always in your best interests to keep moving and always be on the lookout for alternative streams of revenue. These could come from expansion into the realm of online retail or from other sources.

DIVERSIFICATION – BIG NEWS

The newspaper industry is a great example of how companies, when threatened by the Internet have had to start looking for alternative revenue streams beyond their traditional newspaper sales and advertising model.

While many newspapers' circulations and advertising revenues are in decline they are still able (for the time being at least) to capitalise on the strength of their brands and the communities they serve (people still read newspaper content, they just don't pay for it like they used to).

Take a look at The Guardian newspaper's website (http://www.theguardian.com) and you will see that the company now makes money via a number of different channels. You probably won't be surprised to learn that many of these new avenues of business are conducted online.

You can now book your summer holiday, learn a new life skill, buy an eBook, network with like-minded individuals and even find true love under The Guardian's banner masthead. While The Guardian will either outsource many of these activities (often as part of affiliate partnerships) they still carry the weight, authority and perceived quality of a service offered by a long-established and well-known brand.

The Guardian newspaper might be in the business of news, but its revenues (much needed these days in the publishing industry) come from many sources.

FLYING A DIFFERENT ROUTE

Budget airlines are another example of companies who look to different business models to generate huge profits. It might surprise you that a company like Ryanair makes very little money from ticket sales (in fact it probably loses money on its cheapest fares). Most of their revenues come from in-flight sales of food, drink and other products such as scratch cards and electronic cigarettes. You might suggest that Ryanair is not actually an airline, it is a retailer and a very profitable one at that.

IDENTIFYING NEW REVENUE GENERATING OPPORTUNITIES

The best revenue generating schemes will solve problems for your existing client base or bring new customers into your premises.

Examples of this can already be seen on the high street.

A company offering a personal service (such as a hair stylist or beauty salon) might want to expand their offering by retailing complimentary products (shampoos, creams, accessories, etc.). A local pub could stock a range of everyday essentials (such as milk, coffee, toiletries, etc.) providing a valuable after hours service when local shops have closed for the night. A fashion retailer could offer an alteration service, giving a bespoke service to off-the-peg customers.

EATING MY OWN DOG FOOD

As a writer, it would be too easy to stay confined to my garret and plead poverty (unless your name is JK Rowling it can be difficult to make a living from the written word) and so I am always on the lookout for additional streams of revenue with public speaking and private consultancy work being my most lucrative outlets. As an experienced marketer, I adopt a wide range of online tools including social media, email marketing and content marketing to monetise my craft.

EVEN THE BIG GUYS ARE DOING IT

You would think the high street bookseller Waterstones's business is threatened by Amazon and their ubiquitous Kindle device (and you'd be right – there's a really good chance you are reading this book on one after all). But instead of hiding their heads in the sand, they got some skin in the game and started selling Kindles on behalf of the Internet retailer, taking a percentage on sales generated from the devices and encouraging first-time eReaders into their bricks and mortar shops. Perhaps this is a good example of keeping your friends close and your enemies closer.

CHAPTER 10 - BACK IN THE REAL WORLD

And so we finish this book back in the real world. As real world business continues along a path that is constantly threatened by uncertainties in the economy, changes on the high street and rapid disruption from the Internet and digital economy, life isn't going to get any easier for businesses that are not willing (or unable) to embrace change.

The ever quickening pace of technology means the challenge of staying current will not be an easy task, but as entrepreneurs we should at least be excited by the challenges presented by modern technology.

Understanding the need to change (rather than desperately protecting a glorious past) is a vital first step to not only survive, but thrive on today's digitally enhanced high street.

If you would like to talk to me further about your business's future on the high street, let's connect on Twitter @john_w_hayes.

NOTES:

www.ingramcontent.com/pod-product-compliance
Lightning Source LLC
Chambersburg PA
CBHW051720170526
45167CB00002B/732